Strategic Enterprise Management Systems

Tools for the 21st century

Martin Fahy

Copyright CIMA 2001
First published in 2001 by:
The Chartered Institute of Management Accountants
26 Chapter Street
London SW1P 4NP
ISBN 1 85971 494 3

Printed in Great Britain

Contents

For Sophie

Preface

The last twelve months has seen the emergence of strategic enterprise management (SEM) software offerings from a number of enterprise resource planning (ERP) vendors. As currently conceived by the major vendors SEM is designed to improve the effectiveness of strategic management processes by providing managers with business performance monitoring, consolidation, and data warehousing/business intelligence capability. Alongside this data and information management capability vendors, such as SAP and PeopleSoft®, are also attempting to include techniques such as shareholder value management, balanced scorecard and activity-based management as part of their SEM offerings. Over the next eighteen months SEM is likely to become an established part of the corporate lexicon. In particular the coming months will see a plethora of management conferences, and technology offerings centred on SEM. SEM systems will sit on top of the ERP systems widely introduced in the early 1990s by large corporations.

While ERP systems have helped to improve efficiency in big companies by using a set of system applications, which deploy existing industry best practices they work at an operational, rather than a strategic, level. They do not show how a business can best create value for customers and meet its objectives, from maximising shareholder value to fulfilling responsibilities to employees, business partners and the communities in which it operates. SEM attempts to bridge the gap between strategy and operations by making shareholder value the key criteria in decision-making and by providing the tools and information to support:

- performance measurement based on targets for each of the value drivers;
- the integration of strategic, financial and operational information to support management processes;
- transparency across the enterprise and to ensure continuity of information from strategy through to execution;
- predictive value reporting; and
- shareholder value-based business appraisal and decision-making.

The purpose of this book is to explore the implications of the emerging SEM offerings for finance professionals and the management accounting and control activities they support in organisations. In particular the book argues that SEM is not just a technological issue but is instead about integrating best practices in the key management process of planning, decision-making, implementation and measurement to maximise stakeholder value. While technology and systems are a vital enabler this book will attempt to show that the successful implementation of SEM requires a much wider perspective than many practitioners have suggested to date.

Glossary

ABC	activity-based costing
ABM	activity-based management
AICPA	American Institute of Certified Public Accountants
B2B	business to business
B2C	business to consumer
B2E	business to employee
BI	business intelligence
BPR	business process re-engineering
CART	classification and regression tree
CEO	chief executive officer
CFO	chief financial officer
CFROI	cash flow return on investment
CHAID	chi-squared automatic interaction detection
CIM	computer integrated manufacturing
CIMA	Chartered Institute of Management Accountants
CPG	consumer packaged goods
CRM	customer relationship management
CVA	cash value added
DBMS	database management system
DCF	discounted cash flow
DLH	direct labour hours
DSS	decision support systems
DV	data visualisation
EIS	executive information systems
EMEA	Europe, Middle East and Africa
ERP	enterprise resource planning
ETL	extraction, transformation and loading [software]
EVA	economic value added
GAAP	generally accepted accounting practice
IMA	Institute of Management Accountants [US]
IS	information systems
IT	information technology
MBO	management by objectives
MNC	multinational corporation

OCFD	operating cash flow demand
ODBC	open database connectivity
OLAP	on-line analytic processing
P&L	profit and loss
PC	personal computer
PV	present value
PwC	PricewaterhouseCoopers
R&D	research and development
RDBMS	relational database management system
ROA	return on assets
ROCE	return on capital employed
ROI	return on investment
RONA	return on net assets
SBU	strategic business unit
SEM	strategic enterprise management
SVA	shareholder value analysis
SVM	shareholder value management
TQM	total quality management
VBM	value-based management
VCA	value chain analysis
WACC	weighted average cost of capital

Biography

Martin Fahy is a senior lecturer in Accounting and Information Systems at National University of Ireland, Galway. He is a Chartered Accountant and holds a PhD in informatics from UCC. Prior to joining NUI, Galway he worked as a management consultant with KPMG.

Martin has written extensively on the areas of Business Information Systems, ERP systems and emerging issues in E-Business and Accounting. He is currently an adjunct professor at the Universite d'Auvergne in France and is involved in research in the areas of Shared Service Centres and Strategic Enterprise Management. In addition to his academic work he consults to a number of Big 5 firms and start up companies.

Acknowledgements

Every effort has been made to contact the holders of copyright material, but if any here have been inadvertently overlooked, the publishers will be pleased to make the necessary arrangements at the first opportunity.

Chapter 2

Figure 2.2: From 'Capability: Value-based management' by Dan Springer, Director, KPMG Consulting. Reproduced by kind permission.
Figure 2.4: From 'Human information procession decision style theory and accounting information systems' by MJ Driver and TJ Mock, *Accounting Review*, July 1975, pp. 490-508. Reproduced by kind permission of the authors and the American Accounting Association.

Chapter 3

Table 3.1: From the *Third Annual Survey: Technology Issues for Financial Executives 2000*, a joint publication of the Financial Executives Institute and the Computer Sciences Corporation. Reproduced by kind permission.
Figure 3.2: Copyright Forrester Research. Reproduced by kind permission.
Figure 3.3: From G. Ross, *Management Accounting*, November 1990. Reproduced by kind permission.
Figure 3.4: Copyright © 1999, Oracle Corporation. All rights reserved. Reproduced by kind permission.
Figure 3.5: Copyright Deloitte Consulting, 1999. Reproduced by kind permission.
Figure 3.7: Copyright SAP AG. Reproduced by kind permission.

Chapter 4

Table 4.1: CIMA survey, February 2000.
Figure 4.3: From 'Capability: Value-based management' by Dan Springer, Director, KPMG Consulting. Reproduced by kind permission.
Figure 4.4: From PBB Turney (1991), *Common Cents - The ABC performance breakthrough*. Portland, OR: Cost Technology, Inc. Reproduced by kind permission.
Figure 4.6: From 'Using the balanced scorecard as a strategic management system', *Harvard Business Press*, Jan–Feb 1996, pp. 75–85.

Figure 4.7: From H. Evans, G. Ashworth, J. Gooch, and R. Davies, 'Who needs performance management?', *Management Accounting*, December 1996, pp. 20-25.

Figure 4.8: Copyright SAP AG. Reproduced by kind permission.

Figure 4.9: From KH Manning, 'Distribution channel profitability', *Management Accounting USA*, Jan. 1995. Reproduced by kind permission of the Institute of Management Accountants.

Table 4.2: From G. Phillips, 'The future structure of the finance function', *Management Accounting*, February 1996, pp. 12-13. Reproduced by kind permission.

Chapter 5

Figure 5.1: © J.D. Edwards & Company, reproduced by kind permission.

Table 5.1: © J.D. Edwards & Company, reproduced by kind permission.

Figure 5.2: Copyright SAP AG. Reproduced by kind permission.

Table 5.2: From Toru Sakaguchi and Mark N. Frolick, 'A review of the Data Warehousing Literature', *Journal of Data Warehousing*, Vol. 2, No. 1, Jan 1997, pp. 34-54. Reproduced by kind permission.

Chapter 6

Table 6.1: From '*Is ERP right for your company? How to achieve a successful implementation*', one of the CIMA Hot Topic Series, by John Blackburn, PricewaterhouseCoopers. © PricewaterhouseCoopers, reproduced by kind permission.

Figure 6.3: © Hyperion.

Chapter 7

Figure 7.7: From a CIMA ERP Forum presentation by Mark Smith of Partners for Change Ltd, February 2000. © Partners for Change Ltd 2001, reproduced by kind permission.

Chapter 8

Figure 8.4: Copyright SAP AG. Reproduced by kind permission.

E-finance: towards effective finance?

1

1.1 Introduction

The past decade has been a period of dramatic change in business and management. At the macro level we have seen the opening up of new markets, increased competition in existing markets, as well as a relentless stream of technological innovation. Deregulation of capital markets and the liberalisation of many previously regulated industries has dramatically altered the business landscape. Other factors include globalisation, changing barriers to entry in established markets (e.g. Internet) and compressed product lifecycles. While many of these forces have led to positive benefits and increased wealth creation, it is important to recognise that it has also led to an extraordinarily high level of mortality in modern corporations. One third of the 1980 *Fortune* 500 companies had disappeared by 1993. It is estimated that one third of today's top 500 will have disappeared in ten years time. With such a high rate of attrition firms are constantly struggling to re-invent themselves and compete in the global market.

Business models, which were once expected to last for as long as ten years, nowadays will last for approximately five years and this is decreasing all the time. Soon that time span will have shrunk to three or even two years. Businesses that do not change quickly enough will become uncompetitive. Shorter windows of opportunity and the emergence of speed/time as a competitive dimension have led to a situation where managers are expected to make and implement decisions in shorter and shorter time periods. At the same time managers are faced with a deluge of information from both inside and outside the organisation. While the systems which organisations have implemented in the past have been effective in providing the hard quantitative information needed for operational control, they have been of limited value in supporting the activities of senior managers. As a result senior executives find themselves 'data rich and information poor'. In these circumstances the overwhelming volumes of irrelevant and mainly quantitative data threatens to overwhelm managers' ability to respond effectively to the challenges they face.

It seems that it is the optimisation of capital, not labour, that is now the route to increased productivity; flexibility now confers more advantage than scale; mass production is giving way to customisation of goods and services; autocracy in the workplace is giving way to participation; and at the same time there is a relentless process of international standardisation. Driven by competitive, ideological and technological factors, all management practices, tools and techniques are converging globally. The only fundamental source of competitive advantage that remains appears to be strategy, operationalised through strategic management.

Organisational structures can no longer be assumed to be one-dimensional configurations. In everyday practice we can visibly see that organisations have moved from the hierarchical organisational structure based on the business functions toward a two-dimensional or multi-dimensional structure (be it by product, region, sector, etc.). These multi-dimensional, constantly changing organisational structures place increasing demands on the contemporary planning and co-ordination process. But the processes operating within these structures are changing too. The entire planning and co-ordination process is being characterised by greater decentralisation of responsibility and greater speed.

In response to these pressures, the last ten years has seen the emergence of a range of innovative management techniques aimed at helping organisations cope with an increasingly turbulent and hostile business environment (see Figure 1.1). In an order to continue to create superior shareholder value, firms are challenged to implement a continuous stream of management process improvement and redesign initiatives.

The most influential driver of change, however, has been the growing demands of individual and institutional shareholders for greater value creation. The increasingly mobile and demanding global investor expects a continuous and predictable growth in return on investment. As a result there is increasing dissatisfaction among senior management with the quality of the strategic management processes in their organisations. It appears that growing stakeholder demands and increasing organisational complexity have revealed a shortcoming in many organisations' ability to respond to the increased velocity of enterprise management.

Organisations must now turn their attention to improving the quality and effectiveness of their strategic management processes. In particular, senior executives have realised the need to put in place appropriate processes and systems to support performance monitoring, business problem solving, business intelligence and business direction setting. Under

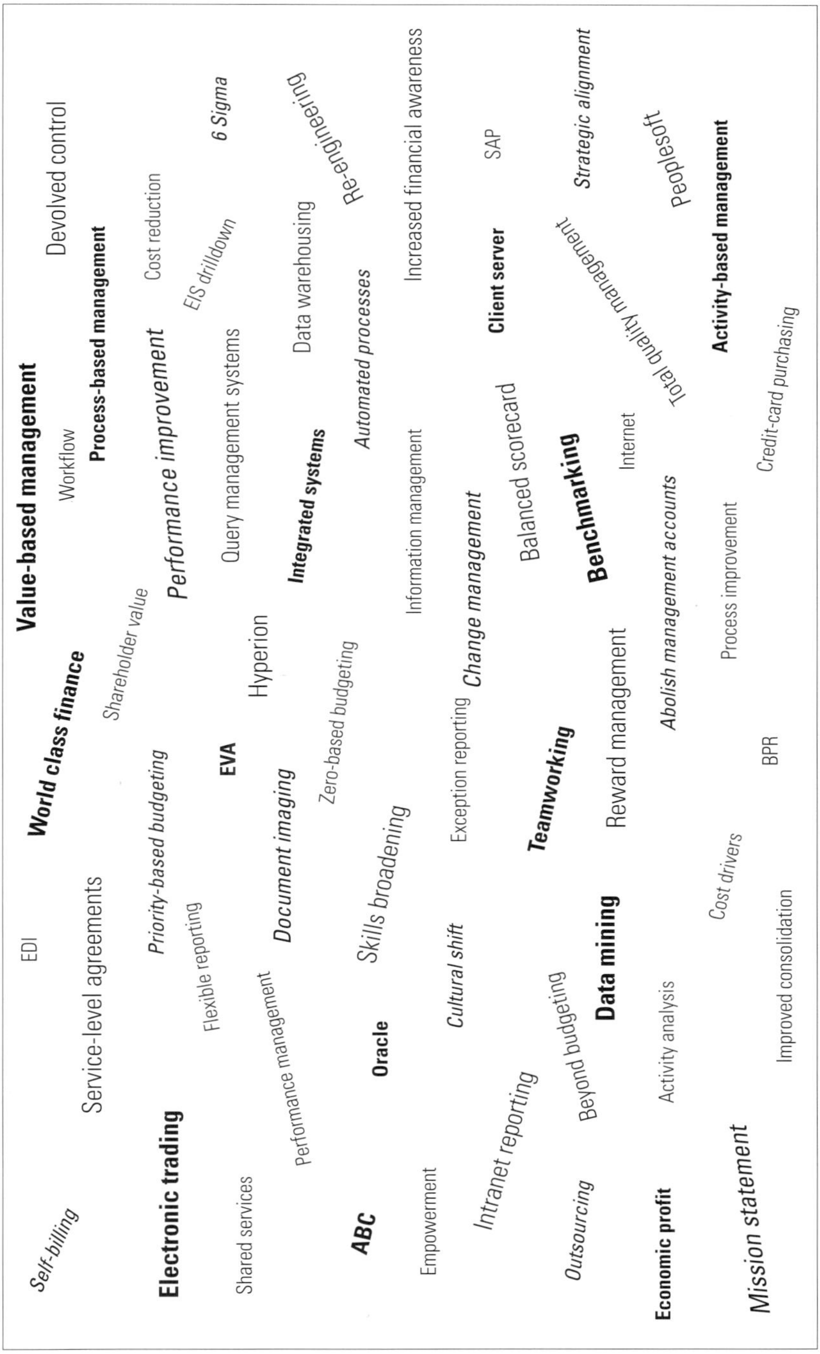

Figure 1.1: The management innovations of the last twenty years

the existing approach to strategic management processes, firms have failed to redesign the reporting and performance management systems to take account of the primacy of shareholder value. As a result many of the systems currently in place reflect a bottom line profitability perspective rather than a value perspective. Thus, the rhetoric of value management is not matched by the reality of performance management and business execution.

The last twelve months has seen the emergence of strategic enterprise management (SEM) software offerings from the top three enterprise resource planning (ERP) vendors. As currently conceived by the major vendors, SEM is designed to improve the effectiveness of strategic management processes by providing managers with business performance monitoring, consolidation, and data warehousing/business intelligence capability.

It seems that the last ten years have been a succession of latest 'hot topics' and firms struggling to come to terms with yet another 'silver bullet' change programme or strategic initiative. Activity-based costing (ABC), activity-based management (ABM), balanced scorecards, business process re-engineering (BPR), and the more recently conceived shareholder value management (SVM), have led to a plethora of management seminars and books on how to survive in the turbulent environment of the new century. Few corporations have failed to escape from the army of consultants and management gurus offering attractively packaged 'solutions'.

One of the criticisms which has been levelled at the emerging SEM area is that there is nothing new in the technologies or for that matter the techniques which SEM encompasses. This is in fact probably true. However, the real potential of SEM may lie in the fact that it is based on well established and widely accepted techniques and maturing technologies. A particular criticism of many performance improvement initiatives is that they require firms to abandon previous performance improvement techniques and systems and replace them with the latest solution.

Essentially SEM is an attempt to improve the strategic management of an organisation by giving finance professionals better tools and approaches to meet the continuous stream of requests for analysis and information from senior executives. In recent years the demands on the time and resources of the finance professional have grown exponentially. SEM tools are designed help/allow finance staff to leverage the data in a firm's ERP systems to provide better decision support. As such it uses a range of analytical applications such as SVM, ABC/ABM and balanced scorecards to help executives manage the enterprise better. In this respect SEM may finally fulfil our expectations for ERP and provide useful information for senior managers.

It is important to appreciate that SEM is not some new magic technology. In fact this book will argue that SEM as a management activity has been around for decades ever since firms began to recognise the need for better strategy formulation and execution. Finance professionals, such as management accountants and others, have been providing SEM type support for decades using spreadsheets, extract programmes and a lot of elbow grease. For years we have seen a continuous stream of decision/executive support type software (executive information systems (EIS), data mining, dashboards, etc.). Many of these technologies were sold as a panacea for all a firm's reporting and analysis shortcomings. SEM technologies draw valuable lessons from our less than successful experiences with these earlier technologies, by recognising the primacy of the executive and relegating the technology to a supporting role. The SEM technology emerging from the ERP and other software vendors is light years ahead of older modelling/analysis tools, however it is still just software. The real killer application in SEM is that it releases finance professionals and others from the drudgery of monthly corporate monitoring and allows them to concentrate on more valuable analysis such as solving specific business problems (excess inventory is a favourite at the moment) and longer term direction/agenda setting. The reality is that the biggest constraint on most corporate business analysis and planning groups is not technology but a poverty of time to think about the challenges facing the firm. Successful firms have long recognised that excelling at strategic management tasks, such as business intelligence and decision-making, is a competitive advantage in itself.

Historically the management accountant/finance professional has been seen as the 'keeper' of the organisation's most valuable assets, but in the new knowledge-era, where many of the assets are no longer tangible, and many processes are automated, this role is under threat. Due to these factors, finance now faces the challenge of re-positioning itself as a value-adding business partner to the organisation, and driver of corporate strategy and new management systems. In this respect the prediction from Greg Hackett, co-founder of the Hackett Group, should act as a wake up call for all finance professionals:

'By the year 2005 the finance function as we know it will have changed almost beyond recognition. Transaction processing will be simplified, standardised, routined, streamlined and automated. That's 60 per cent of finance's current responsibilities about to disappear.'

Gregory Hackett, co-founder of the US-based Hackett Group

1.2 The problem with finance – from scorekeeper to business partner

The finance function in many organisations is undergoing significant change. This change is been driven by the need for finance professionals to make the transition from a scorekeeping role to one in which they actively drive and support the value creation activities in the firm (see Figure 1.2).

Figure 1.2: Finance needs to move to a business partner role

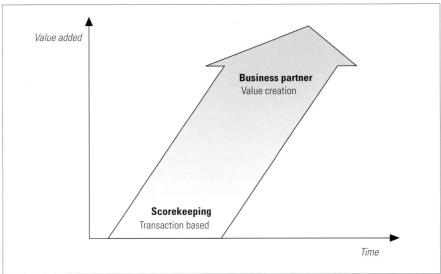

While technologies such as ERP, data warehousing, and budgeting/ planning software have brought greater efficiency to the finance professionals' role the promise of technology remains largely unfulfilled. A recent KPMG benchmarking study identified some interesting findings:

- 87 per cent of CEOs believe finance must become a business partner or leader in the next three to five years.
- Only 56 per cent think finance is already a business partner, and are they really?

- Only 42 per cent of the participants have defined the vision or mission of the role of finance.
- A shift towards higher value added activities has only just begun.
- Linkage of finance processes to core business processes is critical.
- 32 per cent of participants are re-engineering business processes.
- Top performing finance organisations use half the finance resources of median performers.
- Only 30 per cent of finance organisations use performance metrics to measure performance of finance processes.

1.2.1 *The pressure for continuous process improvement in the finance function*

In common with other functional areas the finance function is under pressure to improve performance in the key areas of process cost, cycle times and quality. In particular, the relative high cost of accounting operations compared with other areas has led to calls for greater efficiency and in some cases the establishment of shared service centres in an attempt to drive down the cost of the finance function. While ERP technologies have played a key role in improving process quality and costs, by removing the costly integration and duplication associated with incompatible systems, much remains to be done.

1.2.2 *The need to operate at a pan regional level*

While globalisation is the buzzword of the moment, in practice most large multinational corporations (MNC) organise their operations on a regional basis. A typical MNC will normally have three regions – EMEA (Europe Middle East, and Africa), the Americas and Asia Pacific. In a European context the advent of the euro and the move towards more market driven organisation structures has led to attempts by the finance function to operate at a pan European level. This reflects the need to align finance with the firm's operating structures that are usually product or market driven. Increasingly firms are attempting to standardise and integrate the finance processes across regions. In particular firms are simplifying their statutory structures to allow them to rollout US or IAS generally accepted accounting practice (GAAP) accounting standards across multiple sites while retaining the ability to report in local GAAP for compliance and regulatory purposes.

Firms expect to be able to 'slice and dice' their profit and loss (P&L) and balance sheets by country, by legal entity, by market and by product line. In the past such reporting involved a large amount of scrubbing of data from diverse legacy systems and spreadsheet based reporting. In theory with the complex and very comprehensive transaction coding capabilities of most ERP systems firms are in a position to report multiple views of performance with relatively little effort. The reality for many finance professionals is that statutory and inter group adjustments, as well as local GAAP adjustments, are still delaying monthly and quarterly reporting. In addition a regional or product line perspective on firm performance still requires significant manual intervention by finance staff.

1.2.3 *Improve reporting cycle times and reducing the burden of ad hoc reporting*

In the past finance professionals spent a large amount of time extracting information from different legacy systems and using spreadsheets to summarise and present the information to senior executives. As Figure 1.3 illustrates difficulties arise primarily because of the diverse systems supporting the firm's operational activities. A typical firm might be running its accounting systems on an IBM AS400 while its manufacturing operations run on a separate HP or other platform. In some cases each functional area and indeed each operating site may have had different IT architectures. As a result a large amount of effort and resources is spent trying to extract and reconcile information from the diverse systems. The finance function at corporate or business unit level often spend a large part of the monthly close out manually scrubbing the data from different operating sites and systems. This information is then supplemented with information from external sources and with forecast data. Tight deadlines for reporting typically lead to a situation where there is very little time for value added analysis of the firms' performance. The problem is exacerbated when the executive committee requests 'one off' or ad hoc analysis of a particular issue, such as declining sales in a particular market. This inevitably leads to additional extract programmes and spreadsheet analysis. As a result finance staff in such decision support roles often complain about the burden, which incompatible systems place on them.

Figure 1.3: Traditional management reporting systems

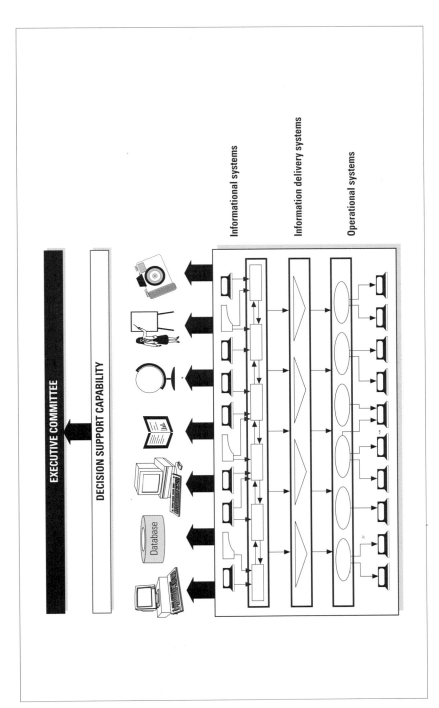

1.2.4 *The failure of institutional performance improvement techniques and technologies*

The last fifteen years has seen a succession of techniques and technologies aimed at improving management accounting and reporting. ABC/ABM, balanced scorecards, SVM are all recognised as having the potential to bring significant improvements in operations. Many firms have, however, failed to get beyond the prototype stage with these initiatives. One of the reasons for this was the difficulty in tying what were often stand alone techniques back to the data sources, which were incompatible legacy systems. A similar experience resulted from technologies such as EIS, data warehousing and so-called 'dashboard' software. While the underlying concept was fundamentally sound the technologies themselves lacked scalability and robustness. Those accounting operations associated with transaction processing and traditional duties typically consume over 80 per cent of the resources in finance, leaving less than 20 per cent for company-wide value-adding activities (see Figure 1.4).

Figure 1.4: Making the shift to e-finance

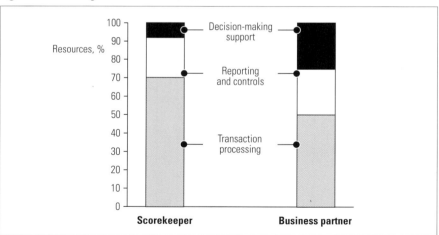

1.2.5 *General limitations of traditional performance measures within the finance function*

Traditional management accounting systems have a large number of short-comings. In general financial reporting cycles are usually closed monthly. Therefore, they are lagging metrics that are a result of past decisions. This means that many operators, supervisors and operational managers consider financial reports too old to be useful for operational performance assessment. In addition, traditional performance measures have not incorporated strategy. Rather the objectives have been to minimise costs, increase labour efficiency and machine utilisation. Traditional performance measures try to quantify performance and other improvement efforts in financial terms. Yet, most improvements efforts are difficult to quantify in financial terms (i.e. lead time reduction, adherence to delivery schedule, customer satisfaction and product quality). In addition, operators find typical financial reports difficult to understand which leads to frustration and dissatisfaction. As a result, traditional performance measures are often ignored in practice at the factory shop floor level. Traditional financial reports are inflexible in that they have a predetermined format which is used across all departments. However, even departments within the same company have their own characteristics and priorities. Thus, performance measures that are used in one department may not be relevant for others.

1.3 Shareholder value – what business wants from finance

In the past, finance professionals have been criticised for not listening to the demands of business executives. So what do executives want from their finance function? The overriding message is clear! Businesses want finance professionals who can help them create shareholder value. To create shareholder value organisations need to design and configure a sustainable business model, and this in turn requires a finance function which can provide decision support and analysis capability across the range of strategic management activities.

For many years finance professionals have concentrated on supporting just one aspect of the strategic management activities of executives. As Figure 1.5 illustrates strategic management involves not just business performance management but also involves the more proactive areas of business problem solving, business learning and business direction setting. For a finance function to be effective it must support all four types of activities.

1.3.1 Improving business performance management

Business executives are continually evaluating the outcomes of past decisions. Under business performance management, executives attempt to effectively link performance measurement and controls to strategic objectives, in an attempt to ensure that operational decision-making is fully focussed on delivering strategic objectives. As part of this approach the

Table 1.1: Shortcomings of management accounting and control systems

- A lack of strategic focus on, competitors, customers and products and the failure to address the information needs of the wider stakeholder groups.

- The absence of the 'balanced scorecard' approach and the focus on mainly financial historical measures of performance.

- Reporting under traditional legacy systems is cyclical in nature and often restricted to batch and month end reporting.

- In many cases IT is a constraint and the firms ability to implement new reporting processes and measures.

- Important business knowledge and understanding of the underlying processes is often embedded in poorly documented spreadsheets.

- With business models and corporate strategies continually changing many firms find that their reporting systems do not reflect the changing corporate strategy.

- Lack of support for flexible organisational structures and multidimensional reporting.

- Poor support for planning, direction setting, and forecasting and too much focus on information for tracking and control purposes.

- The strong financial accounting bias in many management reporting systems often leads to a lack of focus on the drivers of performance and, in particular, the customer facing revenue creation processes. Finance professionals continue to focus on the manufacturing and cost of sales elements despite the fact that in many industries sales and marketing and other brand building activities constitute the biggest element of product costs.

- While traditional management accounting systems were effective in identifying where costs were incurred they failed to provide support for cost reduction programmes.

- Finally the excessive tracking and control focus of management reporting often led to a neglect of, and a lack of decision support for, the important areas of business problem solving, business intelligence and direction setting.

drivers of stakeholder value are the key performance evaluation criteria, and the traditional approaches to performance measurement and control are extended to include competitors, customers, products and relative market position. To be effective in support of this activity, finance professionals must support decision-makers' information needs, provide seamless integration of strategic, financial and operational information and provide transparency across the enterprise to ensure continuity of information from strategy through to business execution.

Figure 1.5: Strategic management activities

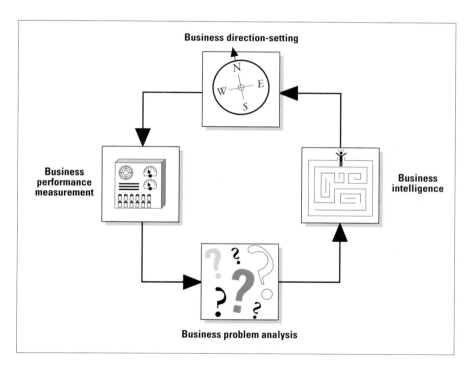

1.3.2 Improving business problem solving

Senior managers in organisations are faced with a continuous stream of complex, and non-repetitive business problems. These problems are in most cases significant in terms of their organisational implications and are often concerned with issues such as supply chain management, investment appraisal, margins, and market share. A key feature of many of these situations is the high levels of uncertainty and ambiguity associated with them and the constraints on managers' ability to predict the outcomes of different alternative courses of action. To be effective in the support of executives' business problem solving, the finance function must recognise that the provision of information processing and analysis capabilities is only a small part of improving decision-making. In particular, finance staff need to explicitly recognise that even sophisticated modelling and statistical techniques are of limited value where managers are faced by highly novel problem situations, where their ability to specify the variables involve is constrained. Finance staff can support business problem solving by providing managers not just with access to the technology and data they need, but by also providing them with tools for improving problem definition, problem analysis, alternative evaluation and choice. In particular, finance staff need to improve managers' ability to leverage insights and share tacit knowledge by drawing on the principles of knowledge management and organisational learning. When finance staff provide successful decision support for business problem solving they do so by helping executives in their efforts to understand and articulate information requirements. They eliminate the excess of irrelevant information that threatens ideas by providing managers with a flexible environment in which to explore ideas and alternatives. As such, a key role for finance staff is helping managers to articulate and make more explicit their understanding of the environment they face and to develop complex mental models of their problem space.

1.3.3 *Improving business learning (business intelligence)*

Finance staff can support business learning by putting in place the systems and processes to allow organisations to effectively gather and filter the information senior executives need in order to make sense of their environment. In particular, finance should be drawing on developments in the areas of knowledge management, the Internet, strategic analysis, data warehousing and other areas to deliver quantitative and qualitative information from internal and external sources to the executive desktop. Finance has a key role in deploying responsive information systems to allow organisations to exploit the increasing velocity of the business environment. Shorter product life cycles, risk and globalisation, technology, etc., have all led to an increase in the velocity of business decision-making. The number of incidences requiring management to make important changes in its strategic posture has increased dramatically. In order for managers to cope with the continuous stream of decision points they need a responsive information system to support learning. This information system must keep them informed of the outcomes of previous decisions, but also alert them to changes in the wider competitive environment.

1.3.4 *Improving business direction setting*

The evidence to date suggests that successful corporations have superior strategic management processes. Successful organisations are those which are capable of charting a course which maximises stakeholder value in the face of a hostile environment. One of the most effective tools of strategic management of recent years has been shareholder value management (SVM). SVM lies at the heart of the effective finance function. SVM seeks to effectively link strategic objectives to resource allocation and performance management, in an attempt to ensure that operational decision-making is fully focussed on delivering strategic objectives. This can only be achieved if firms have the processes and systems in place to give transparency to the decision-making process and to help managers see the likely impact of specific decisions on the value of the business. Finance can bridge the gap between strategy and operations by making shareholder value the key criteria in decision-making and by providing the tools and information to support SVM. As such finance professionals have a key role to play in SEM operationalising SVM, by helping executives:

- understand what factors drive value;
- find where value is created or destroyed;
- establish value as the criterion for decision-making; and
- embed value into the firm's performance and compensations systems.

Fully embedded value-based management takes the shareholder value concept into the front-line of operational management. In particular it shifts the focus:

- from profit targets only, to targets for each of the value drivers;
- from managing traditional functional structures, to managing value centres;
- from historical accounting, to predictive value reporting; and
- from incremental discounted cash flow (DCF) project appraisal, to value based business appraisal.

The increasing demand to create value for shareholders will force management to:

- evaluate its own performance;
- review its strategies continually;
- re-examine its business model through which it competes; and
- implement new initiatives to achieve profitable growth.

The management of an organisation must understand where value is created and destroyed, whether its business model is operating effectively and how this can be improved. This is done by defining and evaluating the strategy, setting targets, measuring performance, forecasting and then re-evaluating the strategy. All of this requires a vital ingredient – information.

1.4 The problem with ERP

Davenport (1998) predicted a number of benefits for the finance function from the implementation of ERP systems. In particular it was suggested that ERP systems would provide:

- Support for strategic planning and organisational change in the form of tighter integration of functions to support management by process. Multiple sites could be managed as a single entity using proven processes.
- Enterprise-wide integration of systems and information through standardisation yielding improvements in data integrity and site head-quarter reporting.
- Cost reduction and revenue enhancements from improvements in management reporting and control, as well as improved efficiency and more timely access to accurate information.
- Data rationalisation through the use of universal transaction codes, and consolidation procedures.
- Improved forecasting for production, distribution and other purposes based on real time integration with suppliers and customers.
- Improvement in transaction processing in the form of better cash flow control, payables accounting, etc.

As an investment ERP has provided an extensive range of benefits to organisations as outlined in Table 1.2.

It would be wrong to think that ERP systems have only had a positive impact on the work of finance professionals. Research results indicate that while ERP systems improve the supply of transaction data for strategic management accounting activities, they typically cause significant damage to the existing decision support capability of the firm. In particular, the introduction of ERP systems will lead to the elimination of many of the existing approaches to management reporting. The increased operational control achieved through the introduction of ERP systems may inhibit the strategic learning which is a hallmark of management accounting decision support activity, and may lead in the long term to a loss of strategic thinking and problem solving capacity at the local operating site level.

Table 1.2: The impact of ERP systems on management reporting and information processing

Single worldwide data repository
Improve performance measurement and control processes across the sites
Improve intra-group co-ordination of production and supply chain management
Replace non-Y2K compliant legacy systems
Provide EMU convergence
Reduced lead-time, improved response time to ad hoc requests for analysis and decision support systems
Improved tracking and control at operational control level
Inventory cost control, job costing
Reduction in clerical, re-keying errors
Time and resource savings reported
Reporting cycle times cut
Better budgetary control and variance analysis
Reduced accounting costs through shared service centres
Better segmental reporting, product line reporting
Use of spreadsheets were reduced
Reduced reliance on extraction programmes and report generation capabilities

In addition to having important strategic implications, enterprise systems also have a direct, and often paradoxical, impact on a company's organisation and culture. On the one hand, by providing universal, real-time access to operating and financial data, the systems allow companies to streamline their management structures, creating flatter, more flexible, and more democratic organisations. On the other hand, they also involve the centralisation of control over information and the standardisation of processes, which are qualities more consistent with hierarchical, command-and-control organisations with uniform cultures. ERP systems offered an escape from legacy systems and their associated Y2K problems to a more integrated system based on a single data repository that supports data mining and other data warehousing derivatives. In particular, ERP systems promised to eliminate the need for spreadsheets, shadow systems and expensive manual integration of data from different legacy systems.

Bob Scapens, a UK academic, found evidence to suggest that while systems such as SAP integrate separate functions and business processes in one system for the whole company, such centralisation can lead to a loss of control at the local level. In particular it was found that finance professionals in subsidiaries of overseas multinationals had to rely increasingly on the company-wide system as the basis for information they provide to their managers. In some cases control over the delivery of local of management accounting information had diminished and this could lead to a lack of locally relevant information or a return of supplementary local information systems.

1.5 From traditional ERP to SEM

For a number of years ERP vendors have been criticised for the inadequacy of the decision support systems (DSS) capability within their systems. Trends such as EIS, data warehousing, balanced score cards, etc., have prompted vendors such as SAP to focus on analytical applications which are designed to support top managers in their decision-making.

With the expanding functionality of ERP systems firms can now get ABC/M and balanced scorecard functionality as part of the ERP. This resolves many of the integration issues that plagued earlier efforts. Similarly the incorporation of data warehousing and EIS capability into ERP has allowed finance professionals to move beyond mere prototype applications to fuller business unit applications.

While ERP is not a panacea for all of these problems or shortcomings, it does provide a framework and the data access to allow finance professionals to fundamentally alter the orientation of their reporting systems away from cyclical routine reporting of historical financial performance, to a more strategic and value added focus as outlined in Figure 1.6. In particular, ERP systems provide the flexible data access to allow finance professionals to gain the richer cross-functional process insights into performance which senior managers typically require.

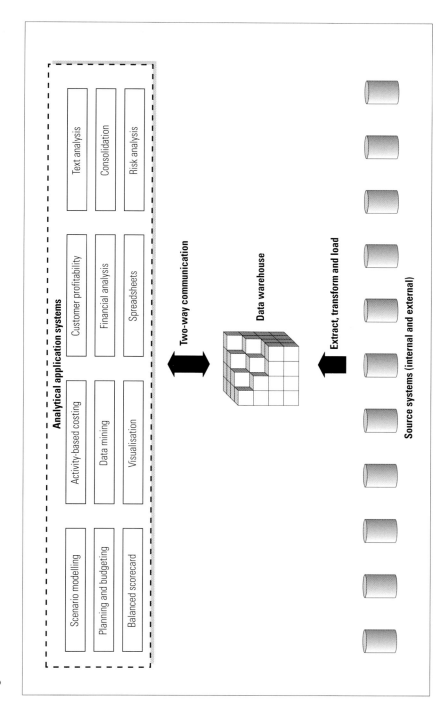

Figure 1.6: SEM architecture

Analytical application systems

Scenario modelling	Activity-based costing	Customer profitability	Text analysis
Planning and budgeting	Data mining	Financial analysis	Consolidation
Balanced scorecard	Visualisation	Spreadsheets	Risk analysis

Two-way communication

Data warehouse

Extract, transform and load

Source systems (internal and external)

With well-designed and implemented ERP systems, management accounting staff are freed from the drudgery of wading through large amounts of data from legacy systems and the manual consolidation of data in spreadsheets. Instead ERP systems allow greater focus on value-added analysis and commentary. Thus the executive committee is presented with more informed views on performance and a more responsive reporting system.

Traditional ERP systems were designed to aggregate data and ultimately to help companies achieve greater efficiency. These new generation SEM systems are designed to take ERP systems to the next level: to make data multidimensional and meaningful and thus to help organisations become effective through strategic analysis and simulation.

Thus, it is an evolved state or next generation solution to traditional ERP systems. SEM aims to extend the principles of ERP vertically to support high level value management processes such as strategic planning, risk management and value communication. This will be achieved through the linking of ERP with business intelligence tools such as data mining, on-line analytical processing engines, desktop analysis and data visualisation software. It will allow for a two-way flow of information, for example, corporate strategists can monitor performance continuously using feed back from the business execution systems, and changes to strategy can be driven down to operational level through new targets and key performance indicators.

Currently there are a number of ERP vendors offering ERP-based SEM solutions. SAP, who are the ERP market leaders, have now launched their SEM application. Peoplesoft® also has its own SEM/business intelligence application called Enterprise Performance Management. Oracle and Hyperion, amongst a technological sea of others, have also developed their own version of these applications ensuring SEM will become a well-established part of the corporate agenda, thus providing the forum necessary to highlight the corporate movement towards the technologies and techniques which make up the SEM offerings.

All of the main vendors have configured their offerings along similar dimensions to Figure 1.6. For example, SAP in their offering aim to provide managers with business performance monitoring, consolidation and data warehousing/business intelligence capabilities. In conjunction with this information-management functionality they also aim to include techniques such as SVM, balanced scorecards, performance management, benchmarking and ABC/M. It has been argued that many of the applications and tools offered by these new systems offer nothing essentially new and simply mirror the functionality that was previously offered in such technologies as DSS, EIS or previous data warehousing technologies. However, it is the processes and techniques that the adoption of these new systems instil into organisations that will possibly be the greatest asset they provide.

At the heart of SEM lies a value creation ambition driven by executives' desire to meet the growing demands for improved returns for stakeholders. Under the SEM approach managers in organisations seek to configure a set of techniques, systems and processes in order to better implement business strategy at all levels of the enterprise. The ambition of SEM is to improve the quality and effectiveness of the strategic management processes by providing:

- consistent data from internal and external sources, as well as knowledge and insights created from simulation and scenario modelling;
- managers with the capability to deconstruct value into its components;
- a flexible modelling and analysis environment to support problem solving and direction setting;
- making relevant information easily available at the point of decision-making;
- connecting top-down communication of strategic targets with bottom-up reporting of performance;
- meeting the changing information requirements arising from dynamics of the organisational structures and processes;
- combining both historic and predictive views to support the entire value management cycle;
- enable strategic feedback to support learning; and
- keeping managers informed of changes in the extended value chain.

1.6 Conclusion

Over the next two years SEM will become an established part of the corporate lexicon. The purpose of this book is to provide managers with our views on how SEM can play a vital role in providing executives with an integrated framework in which to make the most informed decisions and ensure that those decisions are implemented in a planned and measured way.

SEM is not a technological issue but is instead *about integrating best practices in the key management process of planning, decision-making, implementation and measurement to maximise stakeholder value.* While technology and systems are a vital enabler, the successful implementation of SEM requires a much wider perspective than many practitioners have suggested to date.

This book explicitly recognises that there is valuable knowledge and learning embedded in existing techniques, systems and processes and that it is important that this value is not destroyed in the course of implementing new approaches. The ideas put forward in this book will hopefully allow finance professionals to leverage their existing insights and understanding, and augment the value which firms have got from their efforts at process improvement to date. One desirable outcome from this book would be a new roadmap for finance professionals in organisations. This roadmap would assist them in their efforts to successfully deploy the emerging SEM technologies and techniques in a way which creates real value for the firm by improving the strategic management processes in the firm. As such, the book is concerned with examining ways in which finance professionals can leverage existing ERP and other systems investment to deliver on the business partner vision for finance which has been talked about for so long. As such this book has a very simple objective:

To help finance professionals become business partners providing executives with the information and analysis they need to formulate and execute successful business strategies.

1.7 Key concepts

- The velocity and complexity of business is increasing.
- Existing approaches to delivering decision support to strategic management are not meeting expectations.
- SVM must underpin decision-making and resource allocation.
- Finance needs to move away from its scorekeeping role to a business partner role.
- ERP systems have delivered increased efficiency at the operating level but have not led to a significant improvement in strategic management processes.
- SEM has the potential to deliver improved support for senior executives by leveraging the existing investment in ERP systems using analytical applications.
- SEM is not a technological issue, but instead is about creating real value for the shareholders by improving the strategic management processes in the firm.

Understanding strategy discovery and execution **2**

Competencies for the effective CFO

2.1 Introduction

The contemporary business world is characterised by rapid and unpredictable change. In the past our fundamental understanding of the environment was often based upon a linear view of business and economic behaviour, where historical trends in demand, competitive relativities and technology prevailed. The destructive technologies of the microprocessor and the internet have revealed signs of subsidence in the cornerstones of management practices based on the linear, mechanistic, and deterministic paradigm where buying IBM was safe and Amazon was a river in south America.

As the countless advertisements for consultancy and software firms remind us, the rules of the game are changing. In today's environment of global competition, situations can change rapidly and new competitors enter markets with ease. An organisation's ability to evaluate the value of its products and customers, in terms of their contribution to the overall shareholder value of the business, is critical to its competitiveness and long-term success. The astounding growth of e-business systems puts great onus on organisations to carefully manage their chief resource – information. As the volume of information from processes grows, so too does the complexity associated with managing firm performance. In many cases, finance professionals end up using spreadsheet-based financial systems for consolidation, budgeting, and reporting and analysis. In effect, the finance function is failing to keep up with advances in the business strategy.

At a more general level significant changes in management structures, strategy and decision-making have occurred. The traditional passive management philosophy and approaches which had served managers well for decades are being questioned. Increased competition and cost reduction requirements have led to a significant restructuring of organisations. These changes have involved redundancies, major investments in new IT equipment and increased consumer awareness.

Figure 2.1: Strategic view of finance information systems

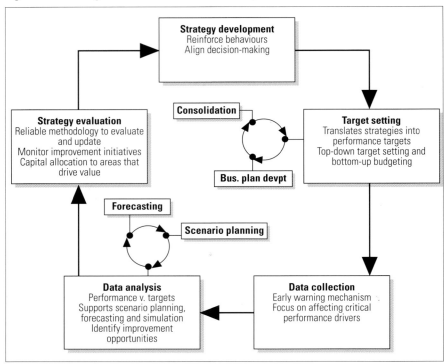

Given these complex and bewildering environments senior managers are increasingly concerned with identifying key business drivers and internal performance measures). Senior managers require information systems which help them to manage the 'key control variables' for their organisation, i.e. the set of factors which are at least partially controllable by the organisation and are likely to affect its medium or long-term success. As such they are moving to finance information systems which reflect a more strategic view of the organisation (see Figure 2.1). These information systems typically include:

- analysis of costs and business drivers;
- indicators of progress towards achievement of a 'total quality' environment in the organisation; and
- information relevant to strategic planning and forecasting.

In addition, senior management's information requirements may include both external and internal information, as well as both financial and non-financial information. As a result senior managers require:

- substantial flexibility in the type and format of information which they can obtain from their information systems, i.e. the types of information which managers require for strategic planning purposes is likely to vary over time; and
- flexible modelling capabilities to enable them to analyse data and information in whatever manner they consider appropriate in given circumstances.

This type of assistance was in most cases unavailable in the highly standardised reports generated by traditional ERP systems.

2.2 Understanding strategy and the strategic management activity

Whilst determining and closely monitoring the strategy of an organisation is only one of the functions of management, it may be the most significant form of management decision-making. The complexity of modern business ensures that strategic management has become the responsibility of a large number of executives and hence they require an awareness of the techniques, processes and technologies employed in operationalising the business strategy of the organisation.

George Steiner, in his book, *Strategic Planning*, points out that strategy entered management literature as a way of referring to what one did to counter a competitor's actual or predicted moves. He also points out that there is very little agreement as to the meaning of strategy in management literature. However he did suggest that:

1. Strategy is that which top management does that is of great importance to the organisation.
2. Strategy refers to basic directional decisions, that is, to purposes and missions.
3. Strategy consists of the important actions necessary to realise these directions.
4. Strategy answers the question: What should the organisation be doing?
5. Strategy answers the question: What are the ends we seek and how should we achieve them?

Mintzberg on the other hand argued in his 1994 book, *The Rise and Fall of Strategic Planning*, that strategy emerges over time as intentions collide with and accommodate a changing reality. As such a firm may start with a particular perspective and conclude that it calls for a certain position, which is to be achieved by way of a carefully crafted plan, with the eventual outcome and strategy reflected in a pattern evident in decisions and actions over time. It is this pattern in decisions and actions which defines what Mintzberg called 'realised' or emergent strategy. Porter on the other hand sees success in being different. He points out that strategy is about competitive position, about differentiating yourself in the eyes of the customer, about adding value through a mix of activities different from those used by competitors.

But what does all this mean in practical real terms? In *Top Management Strategy* Benjamin Tregoe and John Zimmerman, of Kepner–Tregoe, Inc., suggest that ultimately, strategy boils down to selecting products (or services) to offer and the markets in which to offer them. They suggest that executives have a number of primary concerns or possibilities in terms of their strategy. The nine possibilities are:

1. Products offered
2. Market needs
3. Technology
4. Production capability
5. Method of sale
6. Method of distribution
7. Natural resources
8. Size/growth
9. Return/profit

Michael Treacy and Fred Wiersema, in *The Discipline of Market Leaders*, assert that companies achieve leadership positions by narrowing, not broadening their business focus. They identify three 'value-disciplines' that can serve as the basis for strategy – *operational excellence*, *customer intimacy*, and *product leadership*:

1. *Operational excellence.* Strategy is predicated on the production and delivery of products and services. The objective is to lead the industry in terms of price and convenience.
2. *Customer intimacy.* Strategy is predicated on tailoring and shaping products and services to fit an increasingly fine definition of the customer. The objective is long-term customer loyalty and long-term customer profitability.

3. *Product leadership*. Strategy is predicated on producing a continuous stream of state-of-the-art products and services. The objective is the quick commercialisation of new ideas.

Each of the three value disciplines suggests different requirements. Operational excellence implies world-class marketing, manufacturing, and distribution processes. Customer intimacy suggests staying close to the customer and entails long-term relationships. Product leadership clearly hinges on market-focused R&D as well as organisational nimbleness and agility.

No matter which definition of strategy one uses, the decisions called for are the same. These decisions relate to choices between and among products and services, customers and markets, distribution channels, technologies, pricing, and geographic operations, to name a few. What is required is a structured, disciplined, systematic way of making these decisions.

2.3 The decisions – some answers – more questions

Regardless of the definition of strategy, or the many factors affecting the choice of corporate or competitive strategy, there are some fundamental questions to be asked and answered. Strategic decisions deal with the long-term health of the total enterprise and as such they represent a special kind of managerial decision-making. Strategic decisions are those that normally fall within the purview of top management. As such we can view the pattern of strategic decisions made by top management as constituting the strategy of the total organisation. This strategy is aimed at effectively matching or aligning organisational capabilities with environmental opportunities and threats. Strategic decisions are typically highly complex and involve a host of dynamic variables. Specific examples of strategic decisions include mergers and acquisitions, diversifications and divestitures, expansion and retrenchment, reorganisation and re-engineering, joint ventures and strategic alliances, and new product development.

Given the complexity and the dynamic nature of strategic decision-making, it's not surprising that executives tend to develop processes for handling such decisions. Examples of the process view of strategic decision-making include those observed by Harrison (1993), which include:

- *Setting managerial objectives.* Cycles through the process commence with the setting of an objective and culminate when the objective is attained. New objectives initiate new cycles within the process.
- *Searching for alternatives.* Search involves scanning the relevant internal and external environments for information from which to formulate alternatives.
- *Comparing and evaluating alternatives.* Alternatives represent various courses of action for attaining the objectives. They are compared and evaluated using the information at hand, conditioned by the preferences of the decision-maker for a given probabilistic outcome.
- *The act of choice.* This act is the moment when the decision-maker chooses a given course of action from among a set of alternatives.
- *Implementing the decision.* Implementation causes the chosen course of action to be carried out within the entire organisation.
- *Following up and controlling the decision.* This function is intended to ensure that the implemented decision results in an outcome that attains the objective of the decision.

'The essence of strategy is for a firm to achieve a long-term sustainable advantage over its competitors in every business in which it participates. A firm's strategic management has, as its ultimate objective, the development of its corporate values, managerial capabilities, organisational responsibilities, and decision-making, at all hierarchical levels and across the business and functional lines of authority.'

Hax (ed.) (1987), *Planning Strategies that Work*

2.4 Strategic management and shareholder value

The concept of shareholder value is at the forefront of much of the contemporary literature concerning strategy and strategic management. The interest in shareholder value is gaining momentum as a result of several recent developments:

- the threat of corporate take-overs by those seeking undervalued, under-managed assets;
- impressive endorsements by corporate leaders who have adopted the approach;
- the growing recognition that traditional accounting measures such as earnings per share (EPS) and return on investment (ROI) are not reliably linked to increasing the value of the company's shares;
- reporting of returns to shareholders along with other measures of performance in the business press, such as *Fortune's* annual ranking of the 500 leading industrial firms;
- a growing recognition that employees long-term compensation needs to be more closely tied to shareholders.

Boards and senior managers have been concerned with shareholder value creation ever since the ownership structure of organisations moved from the individual to wider ownership. The increasing power and influence of financial markets have driven many companies' boards to regard the creation of 'shareholder value' as their primary strategic business focus. A series of new studies has concluded that institutional investors and analysts no longer rate companies by mere financial criteria alone. They derive their company ratings from shareholder value-based valuation models that are based on quantitative forecasts of the most important value drivers. The studies also indicated that forecasts of operative results of companies are better when non-financial information is also taken into account (Ernst and Young, 1998). Of the 38 identifiable influencing factors, the following topped the list:

- ability to implement the enterprise strategy;
- credibility/ability to manage;
- quality of the enterprise strategy;
- ability to innovate;
- ability to hire talented new staff; and
- market position.

In addition, a close relationship exists between the communication strategies of investor relations departments and the investors' buy recommendations. Sixty-nine per cent of the surveyed investors related the relationship as an 'important' or 'very important' investment criterion (Arthur Andersen, 1999). Both studies point to the fact that shareholders and shareholder value are key variables to be considered when implementing

Figure 2.2: The value-based view of strategic management.

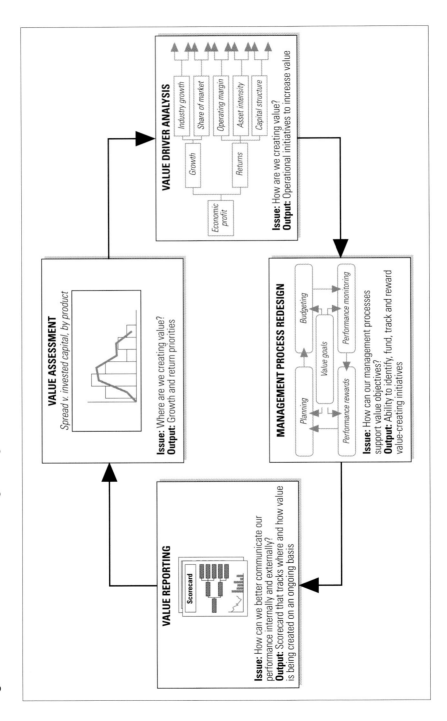

an enterprise strategy. Under this concept a successful business creates value for its shareholders by creating value for its customers and by maintaining its competitive advantage through an innovative business model (see Figure 2.2).

The increasing demand to create value for shareholders will force management to:

- evaluate its own performance;
- review its strategies continually;
- re-examine its business model through which it competes;
- implement new initiatives to achieve profitable growth.

The management of an organisation must understand where value is created and destroyed, whether its business model is operating effectively and how this can be improved. This is done by defining and evaluating the strategy, setting targets, measuring performance, forecasting and then re-evaluating the strategy (see Figure 2.3).

Figure 2.3: Strategic enterprise management

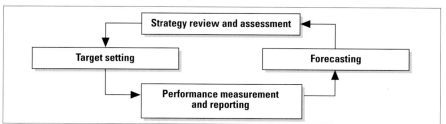

Corporations often find that their strategic decisions are not converted into the operational objectives of the business and that the strategic decisions are not understood or optimised at all levels. Strategy has to move out of the executive office and be integrated into the day-to-day work of each employee. The employee can then contribute to make strategy happen and provide feedback for further optimisation of the strategy. Only then can an enterprise really align its entire activities with the value expectations of the shareholders and other stakeholders, (such as employees, business partners, customers, public interest groups), and thus ensure long-term profitability.

Fortune (1999) cite that it is a widely held misunderstanding that developing the right enterprise strategy gives companies a decisive competitive advantage. In reality, formulating the strategy is less than half the battle. In the majority of cases – an estimated 70 per cent – the problems occur due to faulty implementation.

According to an American study, strategy implementations usually fail to pass one of the following four barriers (Norton, 1996):

1. *Strategy barrier:* the strategy is not operationalised. Only 40 per cent of middle management and five per cent of the rest of the staff understand the enterprises strategy.
2. *Objective congruence barrier:* only 50 per cent of top management and 20 per cent of middle management have a bonus system that is directly linked with the strategy's medium-to-long-term goals.
3. *Management barrier:* 85 per cent of management teams spend less than one hour a month discussing strategy.
4. *Resources barrier:* 60 per cent of an enterprise's resources have no direct relationship with strategy.

Wefers (2000) further addresses strategy implementation failures from the point of view of deficiencies in typical performance measurement systems. He states that from a strategy implementation perspective, typical performance management systems suffer from the following disadvantages:

- enterprise strategies are not explicitly divided into their elements;
- a missing link exists between enterprise strategies and operative business processes;
- there is a one-sided focus on financial performance measures;
- activities are oriented on the past, and are therefore only reactive;
- bonus and incentives are not tied to the strategy implementation;
- allocation of resources does not relate to strategy;
- feedback from experts, persons responsible and information systems is mostly operational or tactical, not strategic.

Quinn points out that the total strategic process is anything but linear. Integrating all the subsystem strategies is a groping, cyclical process that often circles back on itself, encountering interruptions and delays, and rarely arrives at clear cut decisions at any one time. Thus, the strategic management process is not just an 'empty box' that contains only those elements modelled by academics. An additional, non-modelled element is the strategic manager's appreciation of the interdependence of the elements. In particular successful strategic management requires the integration of analysis and intuition, in conjunction with the correct information.

2.5 Where do decisions come from?

As far back as 1938 Bernard contended that executives do not enjoy the luxury of making their decisions on the basis of orderly rational analysis but depend largely on intuitive or judgmental responses to decision-making situations. In a world which is moving towards quantification, most business decisions include qualitative and relatively intangible factors that continue to elude even the most sophisticated mathematical models. Executives frequently couple anticipatory behaviour with intuition and they try to create an environment in which they come up with the answers before anyone is aware of the question.

As such intuition is not the opposite of quantitative analysis nor is it an attempt to eliminate quantitative analysis. It arises because few strategic business decisions have the benefit of complete, accurate and timely information. Management involves an understanding that is mapping relationships between various factors. This mapping is often difficult because of the multitude of factors involved. Harper points to what he calls the paradox of the computing revolution: 'in the middle of the computer revolution, the intuitive skill to sift through all the information – to see the forest from the trees – may be as important as the information itself'.

Instead of having precise goals and objectives senior managers have general overriding concerns and think more about how to do things than about what is being accomplished. In addition to depending on their ability to analyse they also rely heavily on a mix of intuition and disciplined analysis. In many cases action on a problem is incorporated into the diagnosis of the problem. Research has shown that managers frequently by-pass rigorous analytical planning altogether, particularly when the problem they face is difficult, novel or extremely entangled. When they do use analysis for a prolonged period, it is always in conjunction with intuition. In making their day-to-day tactical manoeuvres, senior executives rely on several general thought processes such as intuition, managing a network of interrelated problems, dealing with ambiguity, inconsistency, novelty and surprise, and integrating action into the process of thinking.

In many situations managers simply cannot determine or predict which alternative will solve a problem. In these cases, intuition, judgement and trial and error are used to find solutions. Information about problems may be incomplete but managers must make decisions. These decisions may produce errors particularly under conditions of uncertainty.

Thinking is inseparable from acting, with managers developing an understanding by thinking and acting in close concert. Managers regularly use thinking to inform action and vice versa. In many cases analysis is not a passive process but a dynamic, interactive series of activity and reflection. In many situations managers simply cannot determine or predict which alternative will solve a problem. In these cases, intuition, judgement and trial and error are used to find solutions.

Another feature of the work of senior executives is that much of the knowledge that they use remains tacit because it cannot be articulated fast enough or because it is impossible to articulate all that is necessary for successful performance. As Polanyi (1967) observed:

> 'We know more than we can tell. To be able to do something and at the same time to be unable to explain how it is done is more than logically possible it is a common situation.'

Managers acquire the information they need to function from a variety of sources. Far from being dependent on formal data from official reports, managers utilise a wide range of alternatives including organisational processes, such as routines, ad hoc meetings, etc. As such, much of the insight which managers use in solving complex problems is based on individual and organisational knowledge.

Driver and Mock (1975) suggest that people differ distinctly in the way they use information and make decisions. Some individuals, they point out, use small amounts of information when making decisions, while others use massive amounts. Some individuals use information in a quick and decisive manner, others massage it slowly, deliberately and creatively. They postulate that two basic cognitive characteristics influence how an individual uses information and makes decisions. These are:

1.   an individual's preference for processing either small or large amounts of information; and
2.   an individual's tendency to see either single or multiple meaning in the information processed.

These two dimensions were combined to derive four distinctive decision styles – see Figure 2.4.

The decisive individual uses a minimal amount of information and likes to see the information generate one firm solution. The flexible style uses minimal data but sees information as having different meanings at different times. This style relies on reacting intuitively to events as they occur. The hierarchic uses masses of data to generate one best solution while the integrative style involves large amounts of data but generates a multitude of equally viable solutions. The purpose of a management information system is to expose the significant relationships that will decrease uncertainty in organisational decision-making with a corresponding increase in the utilisation of organisational resource.

Figure 2.4: Driver and Mock's decision style model.

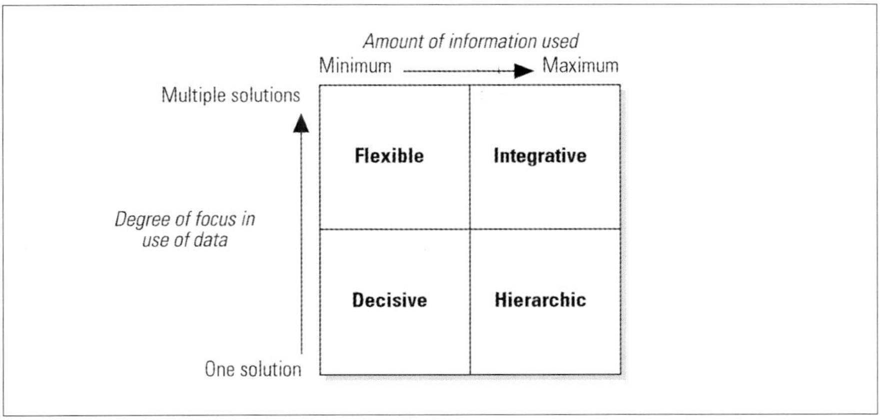

2.6 ERP systems – strategic management information?

It seems logical that in order to engage in successful strategic management the core ingredient is information. As such, since the 1950s information has come to be regarded as a resource of paramount importance in respect to an organisation's current efficiency and for planning for future objectives. The failure of information systems (again including ERP) to respond to the changing needs of managers' strategic information requirements can be traced to the sluggishness of information systems caused by a number of factors:

- the failure to recognise that information is only a small component of the organisational decision process;
- formal analysis of quantified information is at best a minor aspect of the situation;
- organisations are complex and change is incremental and evolutionary; and
- data is a political resource whose distribution through new information systems affects the interests of particular groups.

If ERP is to provide strategic information it needs to extend its information management capacity to include both internal and external, as well as financial and non-financial information. This will require a system with external input, coupled with extended financial capabilities and flexible execution, that can implement one business process today but change rapidly to handle tomorrow's new models, thus delivering more management orientated information.

Despite the fact that some firms are collecting external data, they are not in a position to turn this data in real time into decision-making support. External data is not fed into operational systems and still involves a lot of manual effort in separating irrelevant data or noise from useful data and processing the data into information for use by managers.

A system is required that will, through vertically extending the functionality of ERP, aim to enable a business to systematically monitor and collect data about broadly ranged internal and external business conditions, integrate the external and internal data, and strategically build or extract business intelligence for all adequate levels of management within an organisation.

The past ten years has seen unprecedented changes in managers' decision support expectations and an increasing requirement for flexible management accounting and control systems. In order for organisations to survive, it is essential that their employees share first rate information about their jobs, and that they make good use of genuine empowerment to shape lasting solutions to fundamental problems. A key part of this facilitation will be moving beyond the notion that it is enough to merely make information available. Information must be provided in a way that encourages organisational collaboration and shared meaning. Indeed it is worth pointing out that the end objective therefore is not a smoothing over of disparities in opinion or the pursuit of a single absolute meaning.

The information contained in ERP systems is primarily for surveillance purposes rather than decision-making. ERP systems which form the bulk of information systems (IS) activity in organisations are primarily concerned with the intelligence phase of decision-making. In addition, the categories of systems have a strong tracking and control bias. Support for the design and choice phases of decision-making appears to remain the domain of end user developed spreadsheet-based decision support systems.

By avoiding the confusion and complexity of spreadsheet-based systems, SEM allows finance professionals to streamline their decision support activities and accomplish more in less time, with considerably less effort. As such SEM provides finance professionals with a solution that enables them to provide information to senior executives in an organised and interconnected manner.

With SEM, firms can collect information at multiple levels and roll it into an integrated model. Given that the system pulls actual data from ERP systems, no one has to re-key information into spreadsheets. Executives can assess their strategies using the business models to see changes and their impacts, helping to solidify that all important buy-in from those ultimately responsible for delivering shareholder value.

2.7 Key concepts

- The successful deployment of SEM technologies requires finance professionals to understand the strategy discovery/formulation and execution process.
- Reliable and robust modelling, analysis and information reporting are important parts of the strategic management process.
- Effective strategic management processes can be an important source of competitive advantage.
- ERP systems will not by themselves provide the value-based decision support needed for firms to succeed.
- SEM offers the opportunity for finance to deliver effective strategic decision support.

Strategic enterprise management

3

Technique, technology or snake oil?

3.1 Introduction

In recent years finance professionals have found that the demands on their time and resources have grown hugely. In a recent survey of 3500 corporate and business unit chief financial officers (CFOs), respondents from a broad range of industries were asked to identify the five areas in which their entity is constrained by the lack of enabling technology. The results of the analysis are displayed in Figure 3.1.

Most organisations are rich in data and cluttered with incompatible systems. Some are succeeding in extracting the data that they need to make rapid decisions, by, for example, building 'data warehouses'. However, the majority are struggling. The information they receive is incomplete, defective or too out of date to be useful in making rapid, well-informed decisions about the future. Often they are unable to interpret the data or its implications. At the same time, the pace of change is accelerating. The environment in which firms must operate and its impact on their organisation is becoming less predictable and more threatening. Lack of the correct information, combined with rapid change, makes effective decision-making even more critical.

3.2 Decision support is under-performing

When Forrester Research asked organisations to rate their decision support capabilities, more than 60 per cent said their systems need improvement or are awful (see Figure 3.2). Seventy per cent expect that their decision support capabilities will improve over the next two years, but few are clear on how this will happen. Decision support headaches seem to be caused largely by organisational issues, especially pertaining to data consistency.

Figure 3.1: Key issues for finance professionals

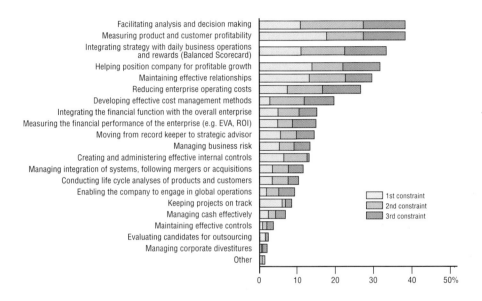

Figure 3.2: Decision support shortcomings

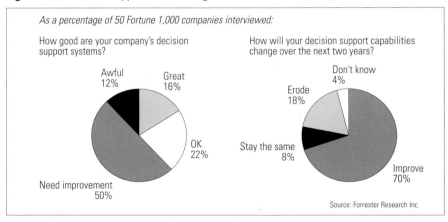

In a 1999 *Practice Analysis of Management Accounting* (a survey commissioned by the American Institute of Certified Public Accountants and the Institute of Management Accountants), almost half the respondents say that compared to five years ago they spend less time preparing standardised financial reports. About four out of five respondents say that compared to five years ago they spend more time analysing information and being involved in the decision-making process.

This new direction in which the profession is headed was predicted by Gerald Ross in a 1990 *Management Accounting* article (see Figure 3.3). He said that in 1990 management accountants were using traditional tools at the operational level in their companies. But to survive as a profession in a new technological world, management accountants would have to begin using more sophisticated tools and become involved at the strategic level in their companies.

Figure 3.3: Where is the profession headed?

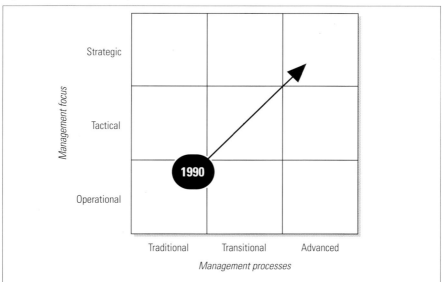

Effective decision support by CFOs should allow the organisation to make decisions that focus on maximising stakeholder value. In order to achieve this finance professionals need to be able to carry out robust, statistically sound and sophisticated analysis using such approaches as 'What if', cause and effect, scenario modelling and multidimensional data analysis.

As finance professionals struggle to stay afloat in rapidly changing business conditions, SEM is becoming the process used to leverage the collaborative strategic management process. In particular it helps businesses answer the difficult strategic questions:

- Which customers are delivering the bulk of our profit?
- Which parts of the business are creating shareholder value?
- What are the real drivers of our performance?
- What do these figures mean? How important are they?
- How do we know if we are doing well relative to the competition?

SEM is an attempt to help finance professionals improve strategic management by giving them better tools and approaches to meet the continuous stream of requests for analysis and information from senior executives. As such it attempts to support the key management processes using well established analytical techniques such as value-based management (VBM), activity-based management (ABM) and balanced scorecard (see Figure 3.4).

Figure 3.4: SEM and the key management processes

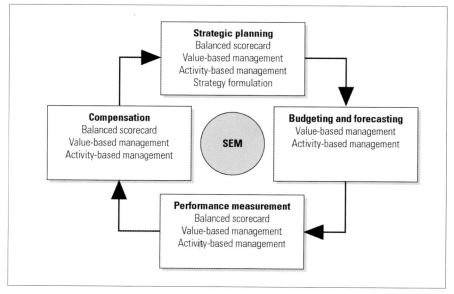

3.3 The value imperative

A recent *Fortune* magazine report on strategy formulation and implementation found that:

> 'Nine of ten companies fail to execute strategy. Only 5 per cent of the work force understands the strategy. Only 25 per cent of managers have incentives linked to strategy. 85 per cent of executive teams spend less than one hour per month discussing strategy. Less than 10 per cent of strategies effectively formulated are effectively executed.'

It appears that firms are struggling to formulate and execute strategies that create long-term value for shareholders. In particular firms are challenged to improve the effectiveness of their strategic management processes and in particular to:

- translate stakeholder (shareholder) expectations into value creating business strategies;
- execute strategy faster and more successfully;
- globally monitor and manage and communicate performance; and
- adapt quickly to changing market conditions.

Planning, budgeting, reporting and compensation processes have been among the traditional mechanisms that companies deploy when managing their performance. Unfortunately these often involve different, even conflicting, goals and measures of success. Managing for value requires that these processes are organised around an integrated set of measures that tie operational and financial performance. It also requires an understanding of the sources and drivers of value across business units and market segments, in order to set investment and operational priorities as outlined in Figure 3.5. A KPMG report on value management suggested that the following are typical impediments to value creation:

- corporate governance bias towards market share rather than economic profitability;
- inability of resource allocation processes to distinguish good growth from bad growth;
- inadequate performance measurement systems, lacking sufficient focus on balance sheet;
- poor alignment between shareholder interests and management accountabilities and rewards.

Figure 3.5: The value management cycle

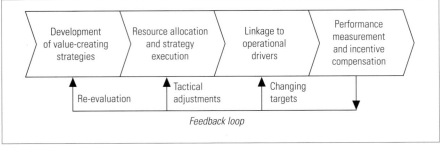

In order to effectively support the value creation process executives need information which allows them to:

- quickly identify changes in the market environment and react to such with new, adapted strategies;
- evaluate and compute these strategies using scenario planning;
- operationalise new strategies using concrete goals and corresponding measurements and initiatives;
- carry out complete, integrated enterprise planning built on top of the target values;
- acquire actual data from different sources and consolidate financial data flexibly;
- monitor goal achievement and benchmark the performance internally and externally; and
- communicate efficiently with external stakeholders.

By definition, strategy is forward-looking, a plan of action. SEM is designed to deliver an accurate picture of overall value creation and comparable value performance between business units, products, and customers, it provides the framework for future action within an organisation. Where should resources be allocated? Which customers should be pursued? What distribution challenges make sense for a new product? By measuring the past performance of products, channels, customers, and other organisational activities, the firm is better able to gauge future performance and make decisions that deliver the best.

Figure 3.6: The strategic formulation – execution-evaluation cycle

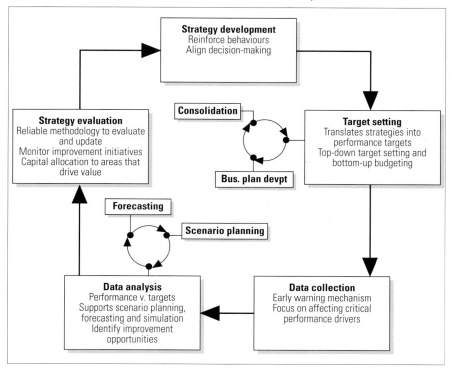

Unlike other types of DSS applications, SEM is specifically developed to extract data from existing ERP systems, and provide high-level, industry-specific and role-based performance and profitability measurement, analysis, and reporting in support of the strategy formulation, execution and evaluation process as outlined in Figure 3.6. SEM is designed to help management communicate strategic and operational objectives throughout the organisation. It does this by providing a real-time measurement of value drivers and reporting on their impact on overall organisational performance. The result should be a single system that establishes strategic performance objectives, communicates those objectives throughout the organisation, and provides relevant information to the people most responsible for meeting those objectives. As such SEM supports the strategic management process by telling managers how effectively they are operationalising strategy.

3.4 The nature of SEM

Most of the major ERP vendors have taken a modular approach to creating innovative analytic solution suites which lie at the heart of SEM software. As Figure 3.7 illustrates the analytical components draw on a common data pool from a business/data warehouse and provide function-specific capabilities. This enables organisations to create their own system, specifically tailored to their unique industry- and company-driven needs. Most of these applications and templates are currently available or are under development by the different SEM vendors.

The data warehouse will normally be the single point of reference for the entire SEM solution. It functions as the central data repository, collecting data from the organisations ERP and non-ERP systems, storing data, and feeding the analytical applications and reporting templates (see Figure 3.8).

3.4.1 *The analytical applications*

- *Activity-based management.* The activity-based management (ABM) application transforms the warehouse data using ABM principles to deliver more accurate measurement of both financial and non-financial performance levels. ABM also enables the firm to analyse various scenarios based on enterprise rules.
- *Profitability, planning and simulation.* The profitability, planning and simulation analytic application will enable management to consolidate enterprise-wide profitability and shareholder value information and extend them into the future, creating multiple simulations of the organisation.
- *Workforce analytics.* Workforce analytics help the firm manage and maximise the return on investment from the human assets. In particular it helps the firm to plan and manage its employee compensation package, including comparative measures. The application will normally also track employee goals and competencies to help identify and retain key employees.
- *Shareholder value analysis.* Shareholder value analysis (SVA) demonstrates how decisions affect the net present value of cash to shareholders. The analysis measures a company's ability to earn more than the total cost of the operating business unit and the corporation as a whole. Within business units, SVA measures the value the unit has created by analysing cash flows over time. At the corporate level, SVA

provides a framework to assess options for increasing value to shareholders: the framework measures trade-offs among reinvesting in existing businesses, investing in new businesses, and returning cash to stockholders.

- *Balanced scorecard.* The balanced scorecard is based on the idea that true performance measures need to account for all financial, operational, and miscellaneous future performance drivers. Their measures fall into four general categories: financial, customers, internal business processes, and learning and growth. Using management-defined rules and measurement criteria, the balanced scorecard will communicate the organisation's strategic vision throughout the organisation. By tracking both financial and operational measures, SEM provides a more balanced measure of real performance.

- *Reporting and analysis tools.* On-line analytic processing, or OLAP, support provides an extra avenue of analysis for users who demand intensive data analysis capabilities. OLAP tools support high-speed analysis of complex relationships and extract very detailed information. Most of the ERP vendors SEM offerings are compatible with third-party OLAP tools, such as Essbase and Cognos, and can provide ad hoc access to data on an as-needed basis without additional IS support or programming for new reporting templates.

- *Planning and simulation.* Planning and simulation represent the most proactive aspect of SEM strategic decision-making capabilities. This forward-looking activity enables firms to use more complete information to plan resource allocations based on activities, current business processes, product mix, and customer portfolio. By altering specific activity variables, managers can also simulate the results of business conditions, including specific volumes, to determine the effect on budgets.

Figure 3.7: The SEM process in action.

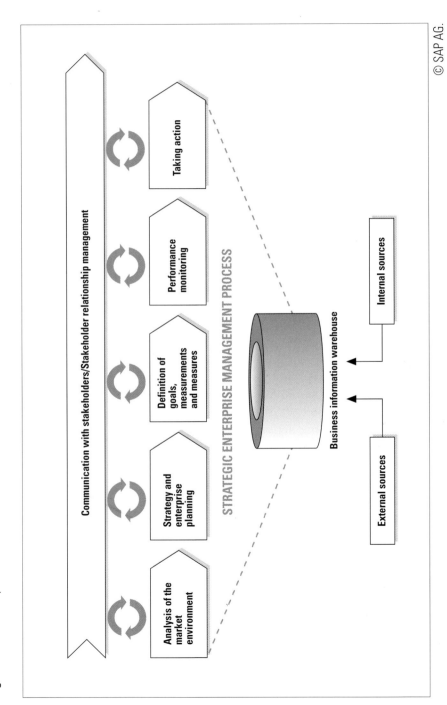

Communication with stakeholders/Stakeholder relationship management

Analysis of the market environment

Strategy and enterprise planning

Definition of goals, measurements and measures

Performance monitoring

Taking action

STRATEGIC ENTERPRISE MANAGEMENT PROCESS

Business information warehouse

External sources

Internal sources

Figure 3.8: The SEM software

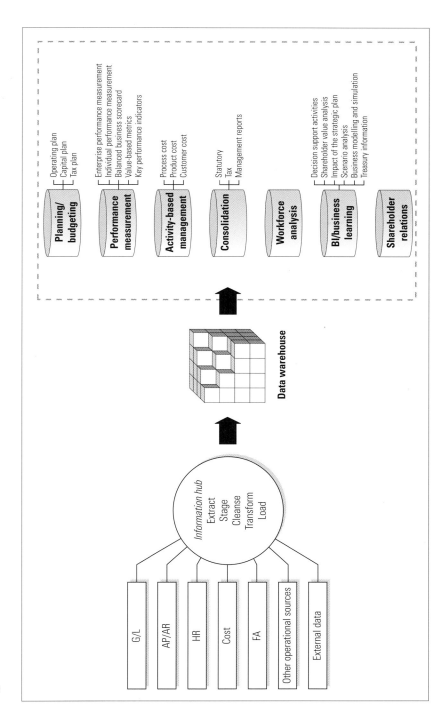

Table 3.1: Some of the techniques which encompass the SEM space

Name	Related concepts	Description	Applications
Activity-based management	Activity-based costing Customer profitability analysis Product line profitability	Uses detailed economic analyses of important business activities to improve strategic and operational decisions.	Increases the accuracy of cost information. Repricing or elimination of unprofitable products. More accurately analyses product profitability. Design new products more efficiently.
Balanced scorecard	Management by objectives (MBO) Mission and vision statements Pay-for-performance Strategic balance sheet	Translates mission and vision statements into a comprehensive set of objectives that can be quantified and appraised.	Link strategic objectives to long-term targets and annual budgets. Track the key elements of business strategy. Incorporate strategic objectives into resource allocation processes. Increase company-wide understanding of the corporate vision and strategy.
Benchmarking	Best demonstrated practices Competitor profiles	Improves performance by identifying and applying best demonstrated practices to operations.	Identifies methods of improving operational efficiency and product design. Understand relative cost position. Reveals a company's relative cost position. Identifies opportunities for improvement.
Customer and market analysis	Factor/cluster analysis Market segmentation	The subdivision of a market into discrete customer groups that share similar characteristics.	Develop customised marketing programmes. Choose specific product features. Establish appropriate service options. Design an optimal distribution strategy. Determine appropriate product pricing.

Table 3.1: *Continued...*

Name	Related concepts	Description	Applications
Real options analysis	Discounted cash flows Scenario planning room for frequent adjustments as new information emerges.	Quantifies the value of business options and encourages strategists to leave	Alternative to discounted cash flows. Deconstructs and reassesses a business strategy Break large, complex problems into smaller, simpler ones. Helps to identify risk components. Trains managers to look for opportunities to increase flexibility.
Scenario planning	Contingency planning Real options analysis Simulation models Strategic planning	Systematically explores the implications of several alternative futures.	Surfacing, challenging, and altering beliefs. Managers can test their assumptions in a non-threatening environment. Identify levers impacting the company's future. Turn long-range planning into shared experience. Develop a farsighted view of the future. Establish contingency plans to respond to changes in the environment.
Shareholder value analysis	DCF/free-cash-flow analyses Economic value added Return on assets/net assets/investment	Explores how decisions affect the net present value of cash to shareholders.	Provides a framework to assess options for increasing value to shareholders. Measures tradeoffs among reinvesting in existing businesses; investing in new businesses; returning cash to stockholders. Assess the performance of the business or portfolio of businesses. Test the hypotheses behind business plans.

3.5 SEM benefits

3.5.1 *Improving the effectiveness and quality of strategic management processes*

The process improvement initiative of the 1990s focused primarily on improving operational and support processes. Techniques such as business process re-engineering (BPR), total quality management (TQM) and ABM have concentrated primarily on improving the primary and support aspects of the value chain. The more important strategic process of configuring and managing the value chain has been some what neglected. In particular, BPR, TQM and other approaches assume the existence of an effective and responsive strategic management process. As the number of individuals involved in strategic management process increases and the amount of strategic management increases, it is critical that the quality of that process is improved. SEM improves the quality of the strategic management process by providing managers with the data, information and analysis capability to explore strategic issues in a richer and more effective way than before. In a new era of ongoing, iterative strategic planning, it will no longer be sufficient for an organisation to revisit its strategic plan a few times a year to compare operations performance against projected performance. As the enterprise and its economic environment become more complex, only the truly intelligent and nimble organisations will gain competitive advantage. With SEM enabling technology, the organisation can develop a highly efficient strategic enterprise management cycle. With leading open systems and web-based technologies, SEM enables business process improvement and decision-making based on an integrated view of strategic and operational information, that supports inter-enterprise collaboration and the best creation and delivery methods to meet customer commitments.

3.5.2 *Strategic management as a core competency at all levels*

SEM allows firms to make strategic management a core competency and to develop a comparative advantage in strategic management at all levels of the firms operations. In the past firms have often relied on external consultants to inform their strategy formulation process with strategy implementation remaining the domain of internal staff. As the velocity of business increases it is no longer possible to outsource the foresight aspects which external consultants bring and instead firms will have to provide this themselves. The time constraints of the emergent strategy approach make the use of external consultants less and less effective. (This will also overcome one of the criticisms of consultants which is that they spend too much time getting to know a firm.) It allows the firm to manage internal processes with an external mind set. Managers thus have the insight of those involved in business execution with the foresight of external consultants and stakeholders.

3.5.3 Institutionalising shareholder value as a plank in strategic management

SEM allows the firm to institutionalise shareholder value as the key guiding factor in decision-making, resource allocation and direction setting. In addition, it exposes the drivers of shareholder value and provides a unifying theme for appraising alternative views and perspectives. This is particularly important in the light of the plethora of business performance metrics which arose in the 1990s. Obtaining an up-to-date, consolidated view of what is going on within the company and external to the company is daunting, to say the least. Linking strategic planning to operational execution, increasing efficiencies, and driving product and customer profitability helps businesses turn change and risk into advantage. Strategic enterprise management supports value-based decision-making by incorporating advanced management metrics and techniques such as cash flow return on investment (CFROI®), economic value added (EVA®), and activity-based costing and management (ABC/M) to derive intelligent key performance indicators and metrics. When these metrics are compared with external benchmarks of industry best practices and represented through corporate balanced scorecards, they facilitate strategy simulation and the monitoring of operational efficiency.

3.5.4 Matching the reality of strategy implementation with the rhetoric of strategy formulation

There has been growing criticism in recent years of the failure of the reality of strategy implementation to match the rhetoric of strategy formulation. In part this can be attributed to the lack of guidance available for strategy implementation in particular the absence of mechanisms for helping firms to operationalise their strategy. SEM provides a mechanism for firms to quickly operationalise their strategy. It does this by communicating the strategic objectives to the operations level in the form of performance metrics and by providing an environment to record the dialectic process, which gives rise to the strategy. It also allows those at the operational level to share the strategic models which are guiding strategy.

3.5.5 *Deploying responsive information systems to allow organisations to exploit the increasing velocity of the business environment*

Shorter product life cycles, risk and globalisation, technology, etc., have all led to an increase in the velocity of business decision-making. The number of incidences requiring management to make important changes in its strategic posture has increased dramatically. In order for managers to cope with the continuous stream of decision points, they need a responsive information system to support learning. This information system must not only keep them informed of the outcomes of previous decisions, but also alert them to changes in the wider competitive environment. In the past firms have relied on a range of systems to support this. SEM attempts to do this more effectively.

3.5.6 *Facilitates the deployment of strategic management processes and allows operations managers to be empowered in a manner which is congruent with the firms objectives/mission*

For much of the 1990s strategy deployment remained the last bastion of Taylorism. The underlying assumption was that those at the operational level lack the knowledge and skill to formulate and implement strategy. While firms were prepared to share the strategic vision there was a reluctance to share the information, models and detailed elements of the strategy with operating sites and SBU managers. Instead operations staff were exposed to changing strategy mainly in the form of changing performance measurement systems. SEM moves away from this surrogate approach to changing behaviour by allowing firms to involve larger numbers in strategic management and by providing a mechanism for controlling this empowerment and ensuring goal congruence. SEM provides the high-level knowledge workers with the tools to support thinking and shared meaning, and the infrastructure to support story telling and rhetoric.

3.5.7 *Facilitates deployment of the continuous stream of improvement initiatives and a performance measurement philosophy*

SEM allows firms to incorporate and institutionalise the range of performance improvement initiates of the 1980s and 1990s in an integrated information system (SEM is to the 2000s what CIM was to the 1980s). Thus firms can avoid the pitfalls of previous fads which often required firms to throw out valuable learning which was contained in older approaches and systems in order to adopt newer processes. SEM allows firms to experiment with performance improvement initiatives and to roll them out more effectively.

3.5.8 *Coping with the paradox of planned and emergent strategy*

SEM allows the firm to cope with the paradoxical nature of strategic management and to cope with the planned and emergent nature of strategy. SEM facilitates the experimentation and trail and error (private analysis) which is the hallmark of early paradigm shifts in strategic management but also keeps managers informed of the current agreed articulated strategy.

3.6 Conclusion

The objective of SEM is to help finance professionals become business partners, providing executives with the information and analysis they need to formulate and execute successful business strategies. By their own admission, finance executives in large companies believe that their decision support efforts are falling short. The problem lies in the lack of a co-ordinated architecture for distributing clean, reliable information. In order to deliver quality decision support as part of the SEM deployment the firms needs:

- a new finance analysis team approach which can build the SEM systems that will provide clean, consistent data to executives; and
- reliable data available in the SEM – and a standard approach to delivering information and analysis to business units to give the single view of corporate performance that they have always wanted.

Executive decision-makers will benefit from this new decision support architecture as they use a new class of interactive analysis to support, real-time decision-making.

3.7 Key concepts

- The future of finance lies in creating value added.
- Current approaches to decision support by finance professionals are not working.
- SEM is designed to support the key processes and activities which encompass strategic management.
- SEM is a new approach to decision support which builds on the success of ERP and techniques such as ABC/M, balanced scorecard, SVM.
- SEM brings key improvements in the strategic management processes.

Strategic enterprise management techniques   **4**

From ABC to SVA

4.1 Introduction

As demonstrated in Chapter 3, strategic enterprise management systems are not just a technological issue but are instead *about integrating best practices in the key management process of planning, decision-making, implementation and measurement to maximise stakeholder value.*

While technology and systems are a vital enabler, the successful implementation of these systems requires a much wider perspective than has been shown to date in implementing systems in the finance area. In particular, a purely technological approach will not lead to the efficient, knowledge sharing, and learning based finance function that focuses on creating value for the enterprise. As well as understanding the technology, finance professionals need to have a well-developed exposure to the techniques which SEM attempts to deploy. In particular SEM deployments will require expertise in the areas of shareholder value management, activity-based techniques and performance measurement (balanced scorecard).

This chapter will look specifically at the innovations in management accounting/performance measurement which are being proposed by SEM advocates to facilitate the provision of the required enterprise-wide management information. In terms of their significance for the development of contemporary performance measurement systems, and their intricate inter-relationship with the SEM philosophy, the following topics are addressed in detail:

- SEM and shareholder value management;
- SEM and the balanced scorecard;
- SEM and activity-based management and activity-based costing.

While separate descriptions are provided, it is worth noting that there is a strong element of an overlap in respect of these issues, and that some measures support others or attempt to achieve similar objectives within the

philosophy of SEM. Each section explores and discusses the issues in relation to current developments and attempts to evaluate the merits of each
topic in the context of practical applicability in organisations today.

4.2 SEM techniques – linking strategy, performance and value

Organisations have long been involved in planning and evaluating their
performance through measuring financial returns, setting performance standards, and comparing budgetary outcomes with plans. For effective enterprise management, this involves the measurement of both overall and
business unit performance in relation to the objectives identified in the planning process. In this way, performance measurement systems are a key factor in ensuring the successful implementation of an organisation's strategy.

Organisations need to understand how well they are making progress
towards all of their strategic goals. Traditional information systems have
been largely based on historical financial performance, but the performance
of the business must be measured over all aspects critical to its success. It
is also important that measurement be directed to influence and forecast
future performance, rather than merely understand and record past results
(see Figure 4.1).

Figure 4.1: Strategy and enterprise systems

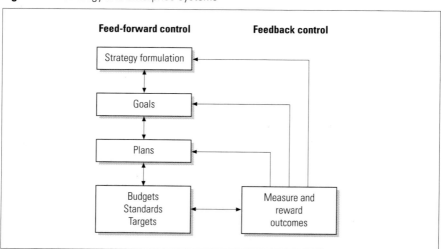

Management control systems are not only important for strategy
implementation, but also for strategy formation. Management control

systems are used not only to monitor that outcomes are in accordance with plans, but also to motivate the organisation to be fully informed concerning the current and expected state of strategic uncertainties. There is a dynamic relationship between formal process and strategy. Competitive positioning, management control and the process of strategy making play one upon the other as the firm evolves and adapts over time.

Performance measurement can only help the business if it is integrated with the management practices and control cycles of the organisation. There is a very close relationship between measurement and strategic thinking and planning. Measurements must be compared with this strategic plan and not merely with budgets. If no coherent, consistent and interlocking set of strategic, process and operational measurement exists, it will be very hard for managers to set useful targets and standards for their employees.

Having the right measurements is vital since the very act of measurement affects behaviour. If measurements are not carefully aligned with the strategic, operational and process objectives of the business, they will prompt behaviour which will run counter to these goals. The way employees are rewarded and recognised can affect the way they behave. Many companies are now seeing the need to develop performance cultures, where it is contribution to corporate goals that is rewarded and not political skill, level or age. To achieve this, performance culture requires coherent direction-setting and performance measurement aligned with reward and recognition support systems.

There is no single set of performance measures, no single basis for setting standards for those measures, and no universal reward mechanism that constitutes a perfect performance measurement system applicable in all contexts. The set of performance measures to be used should be a function of the competitive strategy being adopted and the type of service being delivered. Successful firms will actively use their performance measurement systems to translate strategy into action. The systems and measures used need to be under constant review and changed over time as the focus of strategy changes.

The concept of SEM is to facilitate the modern organisation's need for management information and performance measures that are:

● consistent across the organisation, i.e. there is one commonly agreed 'version of the truth';

- balanced, between historical and leading measures, and between financial and non-financial information; and
- relevant, i.e. reporting on the activities and processes that drive the business, rather than reflecting arbitrary accounting conventions.

The goal of SEM is to show how value can be maximised and how a firm can meet its objectives. It brings together different methods of analysing information within an organisation. According to John Shank it brings together:

- Shareholder value management – where the objective is to provide the owners of the organisation with the largest possible return on their investment.
- Activity-based management – where the objective is to discover what value is added or costs incurred at every stage of a company's existing processes.
- Performance management – where the objectives are to understand what is driving the performance of a business, how that performance is measured and reported, and how to set realistic targets for improvement.

There are excellent and effective theoretical and practical approaches to each of these methods but, while the theoretical bases of each type of analysis have grown closer over the years, the techniques, processes and system tools used to provide relevant information have remained separate, see Figure 4.2.

4.3 SEM and shareholder value management

As previously outlined the increasingly mobile and demanding global investor expects a continuous and predictable growth in return on investment. As a result there is increasing dissatisfaction among senior managers with the quality of the strategic management processes. It appears that growing stakeholder demands and increasing organisational complexity have revealed a shortcoming in many organisations' ability to respond to the increased velocity of enterprise management.

The evidence to date suggests that successful corporations have superior strategic management processes. Successful organisations are those which are capable of charting a course which maximised stakeholder value in the face of a hostile environment. SEM attempts to bridge the gap between strategy and operations by making shareholder value the key

Figure 4.2: The SEM techniques and the inter-relationship

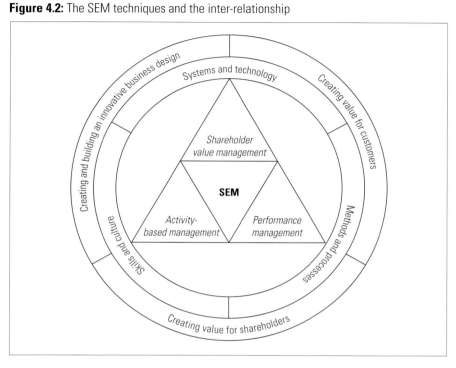

criteria in decision-making, and by providing the tools and information to support the meeting of this aim.

Under conventional approaches to strategic management many firms have failed to redesign the reporting and performance management systems to take account of the primacy of stakeholders. Many of the approaches currently in place reflect a bottom line profitability perspective rather than a value perspective. As a result the rhetoric of value management is not matched by the reality of performance management systems and business execution. This has two major consequences. Firstly, management is not driving the business towards value maximisation and secondly, there is an increasing mis-match between external and internal information reporting systems.

Simply put, the reason is that an ERP system configured along process lines is not enough to enable the new generation of corporate decision-makers to meet their key objectives of maximising shareholder value. However, with ERP as a foundation and using SEM value-based management processes it should now be possible to build a SEM system that delivers the right information, in the right format, to support superior decision-making throughout the enterprise. But in order to do this it is important to understand what shareholder value management is and what it entails for an organisation's finance function.

The results of a survey for CIMA indicate that while the shareholder value approach has its adherents traditional measures still dominant in practice. Profit was the most widely used measure with return on capital employed (ROCE) being also widely used. The awareness of some of the new performance measures was surprisingly low, with 26 per cent being unaware of EVA® and a similar percentage being unaware of the balanced scorecard. Although the CIMA study indicated that relatively few firms were using value-based metrics, it did reveal that a number of them are considering their introduction. Table 4.1 shows those new measures that had been introduced into organisations within the last three years or which were being considered.

Table 4.1: Use of financial performance measures

Percentage figures	Used	Being considered	Not being considered	Not aware of
Ability to stay within budget	99	1	0	0
Target profit	94	3	2	1
Return on capital employed	71	6	18	5
Target cash flow	70	7	17	6
Value drivers	28	18	35	19
Balanced scorecard approach	24	21	29	26
Shareholder value analysis (SVA)	15	13	53	19
Economic value added (EVA®)	10	18	46	26
Residual income (RI)	6	2	53	36

In 1986, Alfred Rappaport published *Creating Shareholder Value*, which finally brought together shareholders and managers with one common approach to measuring company performance that could replace all previous methods, i.e. cash generation, because that represents fact rather than opinion. Rappaport based his approach on five drivers of cash and two other drivers, as follows:

- those that influence 'cash in':
  - turnover growth rate,
  - operating profit margins;
- those that influence 'cash out':
  - the percentage tax rate actually paid,
  - the percentage of incremental revenue spent on fixed capital net of depreciation,
  - the percentage of incremental revenue spent on working capital;
- the value growth potential period – the future timeframe over which the cash drivers need to be measured for evaluation, which represents the companies 'competitive advantage period'; and
- the weighted average cost of capital (WACC), which takes the cost of debt and other equity and weights them according to book or projected book gearing. This is considered more representative than the 'interest' shown in the profit and loss account.

Using these seven drivers, Rappaport's formula for evaluating shareholder value is:

$$\text{Shareholder Value} = \text{Corporate Value} - \text{Debt}$$

where corporate value is the future free cash flow (cash in – cash out) that the company is expected to generate over time, discounted by the weighted average cost of capital.

Value-based metrics are based on the idea of measuring shareholder value by comparing cash flows generated by a company against the cost of capital in generating those flows. Value-based metrics take these value drivers and summarise them into a single measure, be it EVA®, shareholder value analysis (SVA) or one of the other value-based measures that have previously been identified in this section. Whereas a technique such as the balanced scorecard seeks to broaden measurement to non-financial areas and to consider a range of stakeholders, value-based metrics seek to focus on financial performance and shareholders. Such value-based metrics combine the three essential financial characteristics of an organisation: cash flow generated by the organisation, the capital invested to generate those cash flows and the cost of capital of the investment. This feature gives them some significant theoretical advantages over the more traditional performance measures such as profit and ROCE.

Increasing shareholder value should be the basis of every organisation's strategy. Shareholder value management (SVM) recognises that the value of a business is based on its future stream of cash. It comprises:

- development of strategies and techniques to evaluate these strategies in terms of future cash flows;
- analysis of the drivers of value and where value is created;
- allocation of resources to areas that will create value;
- creation of performance measures to measure value creation;
- devising incentives to reward success; and
- communication of the strategies to shareholders to realise the value.

Figure 4.3 illustrates these links in the value management process.

Since Rappaport's book, a number of different models have been developed, all building on Rappaport's proposition and value drivers. Methods have been suggested for measuring value such as market value added, economic profit and cash flow return on investment and all of these will be discussed in the subsequent sections.

4.3.1   *Economic value added (EVA®)*

EVA® is the trademark of Stern Stewart & Co, US consultants, and is a methodology that is growing in popularity, particularly in the USA, with many companies quoting EVA® measures in their annual reports. This model starts with profit and then makes up to 160 different adjustments to cater for the distortions caused by accounting methodologies and management's judgements. These adjustments are based on two guiding principles:

1.   Investment decisions taken by the company should result in assets regardless of how they are treated in accounts, for example training and marketing expenses will be capitalised.
2.   Assets once created cannot be eliminated by accounting treatments, for example goodwill written down in the books will be reinstated under EVA®.

This model is calculated as follows:

$$EVA® = Profit - (Net\ capital \times Cost\ of\ capital)$$

It is supplemented by market value added (MVA), which reflects the spread between the capital invested in the company and the market value of the business:

Figure 4.3: Linking value drivers to key performance measures

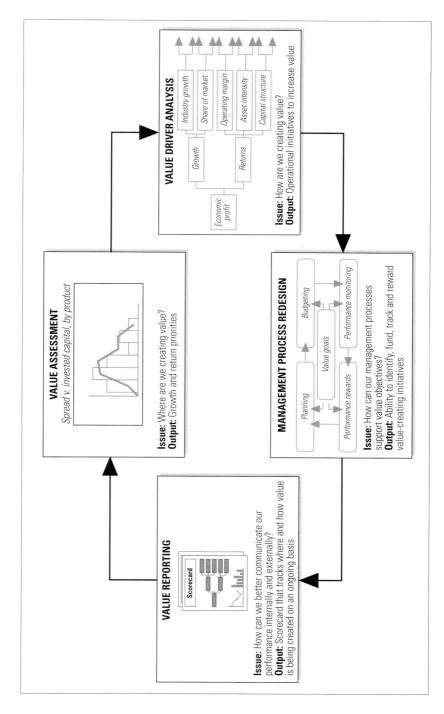

VALUE DRIVER ANALYSIS

Industry growth
Share of market
Operating margin
Asset intensity
Capital structure

Growth
Returns

Economic profit

Issue: How are we creating value?
Output: Operational initiatives to increase value

VALUE ASSESSMENT

Spread v. invested capital, by product

Issue: Where are we creating value?
Output: Growth and return priorities

MANAGEMENT PROCESS REDESIGN

Planning
Budgeting
Value goals
Performance monitoring
Performance rewards

Issue: How can our management processes support value objectives?
Output: Ability to identify, fund, track and reward value-creating initiatives

VALUE REPORTING

Scorecard

Issue: How can we better communicate our performance internally and externally?
Output: Scorecard that tracks where and how value is being created on an ongoing basis

$$\text{MVA} = \text{Discounted value of future EVA}^{\circledR}$$

where returns are expressed as percentage of net operating profits, after cash taxes, to the economic book value of the assets employed in the operations of the business.

Equity capital is calculated in accordance with the capital asset pricing model in order to take account of risk in weighted average cost of debt and equity capital. Companies using this methodology include Lucas Varity and Burton in the UK, and Coca-Cola in the USA.

4.3.2 Cash flow return on investment (CFROI)

Promoted originally by the Boston Consulting Group and HOLT Value Associates, CFROI is popular in the UK as its values performance using similar methods to those traditionally used in evaluating individual items of investment.

CFROI compares future cash flows to the weighted average cost of capital, either as a sum of money or as an internal rate of return. Calculations vary, but they all strive to compare inflation-adjusted cash flows to inflation-adjusted gross investments to find CFROI. Generally, a distinction is made between replacement capital, which is regarded as negative cash flow like normal expenses, and growth capital, which is seen as a genuine investment.

4.3.3 Cash Value Added (CVA®)

Developed and trademarked by Swedish consultants FWC AB, this model has similarities to CFROI as it also starts with cash flow and makes a distinction between strategic and book investments its premise is:

If the average discounted CVA® index is over five years ≥ 1, then value is being created

where operating cash flow demand (OCFD) = annual cash flow amounts, growing by assumed rate of inflation to yield an internal rate of return equal to WACC on the original investment.

The CVA® index equals the present value (PV) of the operating cash flow divided by the PV of the OCFD.

4.4 SEM and activity-based costing/management

An essential element of strategy is to configure and manage the manufacturing, sales and distribution processes in a way which ensures correct product and process choices. In this regard ABC/M techniques have an important role to play. In particular ABC/M supports a continuous improvement (Kaizan) approach to cost management, product pricing, channel selection, product design and other important decisions. Mecimore and Bell 1995 noted that ABC has evolved in three phases.

1. *First generation: Cooper and Kaplan* – The emphasis was on product costing, with the major output being better product costs. ABC made a significant contribution to the identification of internal cost drivers. No attempt was made to examine cost drivers outside the specific business unit. Cost drivers were associated with resource consumption not processes. Activities were viewed as independent of each other. First generation ABC did little to help implement just-in-time, continuous improvement systems, TQM, etc. First generation ABC was a major breakthrough in the thought process underlying the development of product costs.

2. *Second generation: Turney* – Second generation ABC reflected the organisational wide move to a more process oriented view of organisations associated with the BPR focus of the early 1990s. In particular it recognised the inadequacies of functional/departmental approaches to costing and management accounting systems. By moving to a process oriented approach ABC/M techniques are seeking to align costing and cost management techniques with the organisational posture at the strategic level. Continuous improvements are made to processes that impact the costs of products and continuous performance evaluations are carried out. Both first and second generation ABCs focus only on internal activities and provide management with limited information for strategic planning.

3. *Third generation: Porter, Shanks and Govindargan* – ABC/M focuses on the business unit and its relationship with others inside and outside the business unit. It links activities to processes and then processes to a business unit. In value chain analysis the focus is external to the firm with each firm viewed in the context of the overall chain of value creating activities of which the firm is only a part, from basic raw material to end use consumers.

The emphasis in the mid to late 1990s has been on practical implementation issues, customer and market segment profitability, new management and management accounting initiatives, such as target costing and the use of ABC, to solve particular business issues, e.g. transfer pricing.

4.4.1 Activity-based costing

The evolution of ABC reflects the gradual shift in management accounting from mainly operational control and management control activities to supporting strategic planning and shareholder wealth creation. Several writers, but principally Cooper and Kaplan, have identified the deficiencies of traditional cost systems.

A traditional costing system which allocates overhead using a unit-based cost driver, e.g. direct labour hours (DLH), is inappropriate where DLH has fallen to an insignificant proportion (< 10 per cent) of total cost, the range of products has diversified, product complexity design and use of activities varies, overhead is increased as percentage of total cost, or automation has replaced direct labour. Poorly designed or outdated accounting and control systems can distort the realities of manufacturing performance.

Traditional cost systems only provided financial data to management to the exclusion of non-financial data. Non-financial measures are very important on quality, inventory, productivity, innovation and employees in the new manufacturing environment. Traditional accounting systems were designed to produce monthly financial statements to be sent to corporate headquarters for consolidation with little correlation between these financial statements and the actual value creating activities in the factory.

Symptoms of an inaccurate product cost system, identified by Cooper (1987), include:

● Products that are difficult to manufacture are reported as profitable although they are not produced at a premium. If the cost system captures the additional manufacturing costs, then either the products sell at a premium or product margins are very low. In most cases the cost system fails to capture actual costs and instead reports costs that reflect average levels of manufacturing difficulty.

● Profit margins cannot easily be explained: factors that influence profitability are market share, quality differential, production process differences and economies of scale.

- Some products not sold by competitors have high reported margins. If the firm does not have competitive advantages, such as patents, brand names or proprietary production processes, why are competitors not competing for this market segment?

- Results of bids are difficult to explain. If management is unable to accurately predict what bids it will win, the costing system may be to blame. Management should look at bids that were priced low to win but did not or bids priced high and expected to lose but did not.

- The competition's high volume products are priced at apparently unrealistically low levels. When competitors with no apparent economic advantage price their high volume products at what appear to be unrealistically low levels but are making good returns, then the cost system is the prime suspect.

- Vendor's bids for component parts are lower than expected. Vendors appear to be able to supply components at lower cost than they can be manufactured in house. Traditional cost systems are poor aids to decision-making. They fail to specify the amount of overhead that is avoided by buying. They overestimate the savings, thus favouring the buy decision.

- Customers ignore price increases even when there is no corresponding increase in cost. Customers usually react negatively to price increases. If they do not, then the product price is less than the customer's perceived value of the product. This may imply that the product is under-costed.

ABC assumes that activities consume resources that cause cost and that cost objects consume activities. The cost assignment view is a two-stage model. Firstly, the cost of resources are assigned to activities by means of resource drivers which approximate the use of resources by activities. Secondly, the cost of activities are assigned to cost objects, e.g. products, by means of activity drivers which approximate the use of activities by cost objects. Each type of resource traced to an activity becomes a cost element in an activity cost pool. The activity cost pool is the total cost associated with an activity. Related activities are enclosed in an activity centre often clustered by function or process. This is illustrated in Figure 4.4.

ABC is more than just a new way of doing accounting, it is a tool for making strategic decisions and a method of focusing on operational efficiencies. The underlying foundation of all ABC systems is their belief that the organisation is made up of activities. From an activity perspective, activities consume resources and cost objects consume activities.

ABC provides information about the work done in activities or processes. On a more detailed level the process view provides information about cost drivers and about performance measures for each activity or process in the customer chain. Much of the information is non-financial in nature.

Figure 4.4: The cost assignment view of ABC – Turney (1991a)

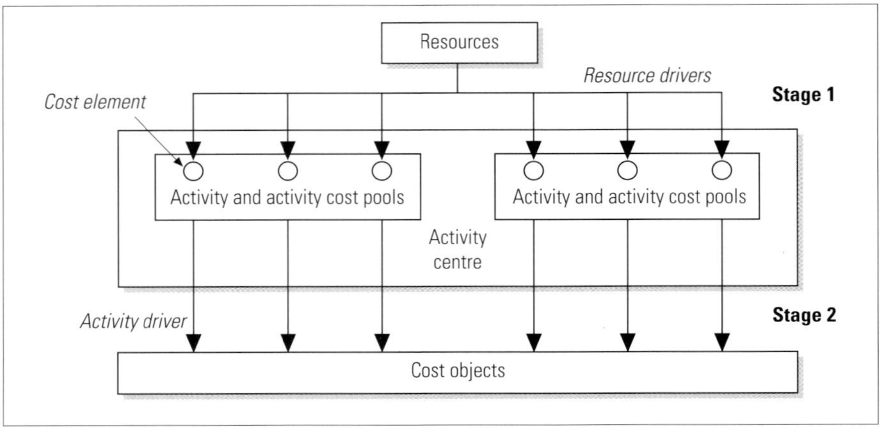

4.4.2 Activity-based management

ABM is a logical extension of ABC. Turney did much of the groundbreaking work in this area. His book *Common Cents – the ABC Performance Breakthrough* was published in 1991. ABM involves using ABC to improve a business. ABC information helps ABM direct resources to activities that yield the greatest profitability and helps improve the way work is carried out. This is achieved through *activity analysis, cost driver analysis* and *performance analysis.*

Activity analysis involves:

● Identifying non-value-added activities, i.e. the activity is essential to the customer or essential to the functioning of the organisation. An example of a non-value-added activity is maintaining independently two sets of bills of materials one for engineering and one for production. Non-value-added activities are candidates for elimination.

● Shifting the organisation focus onto significant activities by applying the Pareto rule. ABC helps identify significant activities and divert attention to them.

● Benchmarking activities against best practice, thus identifying scope for improvement.

● Examining the link between activities. Poorly performed activities earlier in the linked chain of activities can have knock-on effects on other activities later in the chain. For example, purchase orders generated by the purchasing department with incorrect prices result in extra non-essential work in the accounts payable department during the activity which requires that they match the invoice price to the purchase order price prior to approving payment.

Cost driver analysis involves searching for those things that require a company to perform non-essential activities or to perform activities below par. For example, moving product internally between two processes is a non-value-added activity. Corrective action is to reorganise the plant such that the two processes are side by side in sequence.

Performance analysis is concerned with fostering improvement in the right areas. To do this the organisation must determine its key objectives, communicate these objectives to the people in the organisation, and finally develop measures to access the performance of each activity. These measures should signify how each activity contributes to the overall mission.

Turney 1991 noted that ABM has two goals: (a) to improve the value received by customers and (b) to improve profits by providing this value. Customers want products and services that fit a specific need, they want quality and service, an affordable price, they want to be *delighted* and they want it now. In providing customer value, a firm must also provide an adequate return on stockholder investment. Company profitability is important to the customer in the long run: they want the company around for the long haul.

A company does this in two ways:

1. *Improving strategic position:* A successful business deploys resources to those activities that yield the highest strategic benefit. Taking a strategic choice determines the activities and resources needed. The firm must analyse the link between its strategy and the activities and resources needed to put the strategy into place.

2. *Improving strategic capability:* Improve what matters to the customer. Improving activity performance has three steps:
   - analyse activities to identify opportunities for improvement;
   - dig for drivers – the factors that cause waste; and
   - measure the things an activity should be doing well if it contributes to an organisation's success and the profitable servicing of its customers.

Both these goals are achieved through the management of activities. Each activity makes a measurable contribution to improving customer value through improved quality, timeliness, reliable delivery, or low cost. Managing activities is a process of relentless and continuous improvement of all aspects of the business.

Continuing improvements to processes and products leading to increased customer satisfaction and higher profits is a key goal of ABM. Continuous improvement of products means designing products that meet customer requirements yet are easier and faster to manufacture, e.g. products designed with modular subassemblies and a common chassis can be assembled on the same production line. Continuous improvement of processes means the ongoing search for waste in operating activities and the elimination of this waste, e.g. reducing set-up time on a machine reduces cost and improves flexibility and quality.

Achieving cost reduction can be done in four ways:

1. *Activity reduction* focuses on reducing the elapsed time and effort required to perform activities and translates into a reduction in resource requirements.
2. *Activity elimination* where changes to the production process or products can eliminate the need to perform activities.
3. *Activity selection.* A product or process can be designed in several ways with each activity having its own set of activities and associated cost. Design for cost reduction involves choosing a low cost alternative from several competing alternatives.
4. *Activity sharing.* The designer of a product or process can choose design alternatives that permit products to share activities. Sharing activities provides economics of scale in using these activities.

Each of these can be achieved by (a) redesigning the product or (b) redesigning the process.

In each case ABC is superior to conventional costing as it facilitates identification of activities to be targeted for cost reduction.

4.4.3 Activity-based techniques – the SEM case

Activity-based techniques can help an organisation by:

● increasing the value the customer receives from consuming goods and services; and

- increasing and sustaining organisational profitability by discovering what value is added, or costs incurred, at every stage of a company's processes.

What is different about this approach is that it makes shareholder value targets meaningful to front line managers. The individuals responsible for pieces of the organisational pie, logistics, manufacturing, sales and finance, all know precisely what they must do to deliver their specific targets. Hope and Hope point out that this type of information focuses the attention of managers on the underlying causes, or drivers, of cost and profit on the premise that people cannot manage costs, they can only manage activities that cause costs.

ABM reshapes how companies manage costs. By understanding its activities, a company can expose opportunities for performance improvement that conventional cost accounting systems seldom detect. Cost management is improved by identifying what the organisation does and providing a benchmark to judge how much better a company's performance might be. Also, product cost accuracy is enhanced by more discrete tracing of activities to products. Nowadays the primary issues in ABC/M are not technical or accounting issues, but involve gaining insights into the organisations activities, processes and competitive environment and building a business/cost model that reflects the changing reality of the firm (see Figure 4.5).

Implementation is not simple and not quick. Problems that an organisation may consider include:

- difficulties in assigning costs to activities that reflect true causation;
- difficulties in identifying and selecting cost drivers;
- inadequate computer software;
- difficulties in defining distinct activities;
- lack of adequate resources;
- difficulties in selling the concept of ABC to managers; and
- lack of internal expertise.

In addition the large volume of data needed, the cost of collecting the data and the high maintenance costs in updating data are further potential problems. The sheer volume of information can lead to complexity, resulting in report reconciliation and even a reversion to traditional reporting. The literature also needs to consider the behavioural aspects of implementing ABC/M in more depth. Thus, while ABC/M has been a significant step forward in the search for more accurate product costs, it has not

Figure 4.5: Outputs of SEM ABM

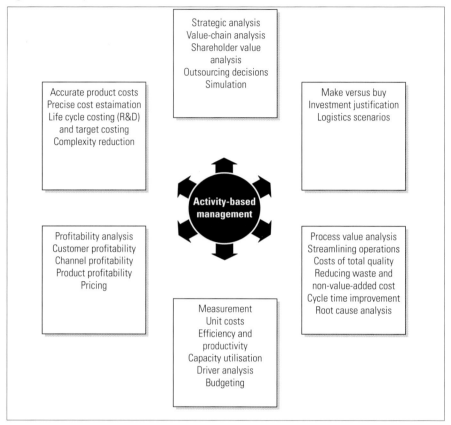

proved to be the panacea its advocates first suggested. The application of ABC systems frequently runs into problems of data collection and lack of integration with the financial system.

Kaplan and Cooper (1998) claim that one of the most important benefits of balanced, integrated systems occurs when managers use their cost systems on a prospective basis, e.g. as part of the financial budgeting process. ABC gives organisations the opportunity to move from static to dynamic budgeting. Instead of authorising the supply of resources in forthcoming periods based on historical spending patterns, managers can supply resources based on the anticipated demands for activities that they expect will be performed. When ABC is used proactively in the budgeting process, it does away with conventional thinking about fixed and variable costs. It gives managers the information they need to make almost all organisational expenses variable.

4.5 SEM and the balanced scorecard/performance measurement

For several years, senior executives have been rethinking how to measure the performance of their business. They have recognised that new strategies and competitive realities demand new measurement systems. Now they are deeply engaged in defining and developing those systems for their companies. At the heart of the revolution lies a radical decision: to shift from treating financial figures as the foundation for performance measurement to treating them as one among a broader set of measures.

Many people now believe that traditional performance measures are inadequate and can sometimes be misleading. They are inflexible, and produce information that is often too late to be effective. Authors, such as Hussain (1996), argue that financial measures are not meaningful in the control of production or distribution activities, and factory operators do not think in terms of the financial aspects of their work. Performance measures need to be aligned with the organisation's strategy.

Strategy is implemented as a result of continuous decision-making at all levels of the business. Firms need to ensure that the processes are in place so that daily actions, weekly tactical operational decisions, and monthly departmental actions are coherent and driven by strategy. In addition the information systems should be able to gather, synthesise and communicate the right information to the right people at the right time. This information should reflect the complexity of the business and of the type of decisions which are required. Much broader, more forward-looking information systems are needed for value-based decision-making. In these systems, external data can be balanced with internal data, predictive with historical data, and financial with non-financial data. As managers try to remedy the inadequacies of current performance measurement systems, some have focused on making financial measures more relevant. Others have focused on improving operational measures, arguing that the financial results will follow. Kaplan and Norton (1992) argue that managers should not have to choose between the two approaches as no single measure can provide a clear performance target or focus attention on the critical areas of the business. Their view is that managers need a balanced presentation of both financial and operational measures. They liken it to the dials and indicators of an aeroplane cockpit, i.e. pilots need detailed information about many aspects of the flight. Similarly, the complexity of managing an organisation today requires that managers be able to view performance in several areas simultaneously. The balanced scorecard approach suggests selecting key performance measures from the financial, customer, internal processes, and learning and growth perspectives.

More specifically, the balanced scorecard provides executives with a comprehensive framework that translates a company's vision and strategy into a coherent set of performance measures. It goes beyond the vision or the mission statement and translates mission and strategy into four different perspectives:

1.   financial,
2.   customer,
3.   internal business process, and
4.   learning and growth.

From these perspectives, Kaplan and Norton (1992) describe the balanced scorecard as providing answers to four different questions:

- How do we look to shareholders? (financial perspective)
- How do customers see us? (customer perspective)
- What must we excel at? (internal perspective)
- Can we continue to improve and create value? (innovation and learning perspective).

In this way, the four perspectives provide the framework for the balanced scorecard, as depicted in Figure 4.6 (Kaplan and Norton, 1996a, 1996b).

The four perspectives permit a balance between short-term and long-term objectives, between outcomes desired and the performance drivers of those outcomes, and between hard objective measures and softer more subjective measures. While the multiplicity of measures on a balanced scorecard may seem confusing, properly constructed scorecards contain a unity of purpose, since all the measures are directed towards achieving an integrated strategy.

4.5.1   *Financial measures*

Financial measures are valuable in summarising the readily measurable economic consequences of actions already taken. They indicate whether an organisation's strategy, implementation, and execution are contributing to bottom line improvement. Financial measures typically relate to profitability, e.g. operating income, return on capital employed, or economic

Figure 4.6: Balanced scorecard framework

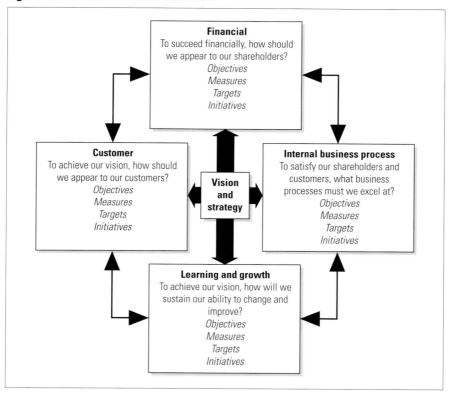

value-added. Alternative financial measures could be sales growth or cash flow generation. The right financial measures for the balanced scorecard can depend on the stage the business is at in the economic life cycle. Whether it is at the growth, sustain, or harvest stage will require different emphasis in the chosen measures. Kaplan and Norton state that financial performance measures indicate whether the company's strategy, implementation, and execution are contributing to bottom-line improvement. Typical financial goals have to do with profitability, growth and shareholder value:

- Shareholder loyalty (e.g. switching behaviour)
- Shareholder mix (institutional vs. individual; employee; other)
- EVA® (economic value added)
- MVA (market value added)
- Net income

- ROI (return on investment)
- ROE (return on equity)
- ROCE (return on capital employed)
- Financial strength: assets (liquid assets), quick ratio, credit rating, debt, debt–equity ratio
- Variable vs. non-variable expenses (e.g. non-operation income/expense)
- Programmed expense – controllable expenses including routine, one-time, and additional project expenses
- Routine expense (e.g. salaries, maintenance, supplies)
- One-time – truly 'non-recurring' expenditures
- Non-operating income/expense – financial impact not directly related to current operations
- Fixed expenses, such as depreciation, real estate and personal property taxes
- Allocated expenses – overhead that is reallocated to business units
- Direct department expense
- Net retained expense
- Major cash expenditures
- Administrative costs
- Profit margin
- Revenue/expense ratio
- Capital efficiency
- Revenue/employee
- Cost of product
- Activity costs
- Revenue generated from customer segments (e.g. new; affluent; large vs. small; industry; region)
- Customer revenue list
- Market share – percentage of market in dollars or number of accounts/products
- Market share ($)
- Market potential ($)
- Increase in major projects – count of number of projects over a specified value
- New customers/markets: number of prospects, percentage of potential deals that are actually closed, new accounts.

4.5.2 *Customer and market measures*

In the customer perspective of the balanced scorecard, managers identify the customer and market segments in which the business will compete, and the measures of performance in these targeted segments. Core outcome measures include customer satisfaction, customer retention, new customer acquisition, customer profitability, and market share in targeted segments. There should also be specific measures relating to the value propositions that the company will deliver to the target segments. These are factors that are critical in making customers switch to or remain loyal to the organisation. These could include short lead times, on-time delivery, or innovation in products and services. Customers concerns tend to fall into four categories: time, quality, performance and service and cost. Lead time measures the time required for the company to meet its customers needs. For existing products, lead time can be measured from the time the company receives an order to the time it actually delivers the product or service to the customer. Quality measures the defect level of incoming products as perceived and measured by the customer. Quality could also measure on-time delivery, the accuracy of the company's delivery forecasts. The combination of performance and service measures how the company's products or services contribute to creating value for its customers. To put the balanced scorecard to work, companies should articulate goals for time, quality, and performance and service and then translate these goals into specific measures:

- Customer loyalty/retention.
- Drivers of overall customer satisfaction and value, including survey-based measures of: brand value, product quality, service quality.
- Customer/consumer satisfaction: market perceived value.
- Partnering index – rating by customer relationship with organisation, including such things as involvement in planning, involvement in projects, investment in product and services (e.g. information technology).

4.5.3 *The internal process measures*

In the internal business process perspective, managers identify the critical internal business processes in which the organisation must excel. These processes enable the business unit to deliver the value propositions that will attract and retain customers in targeted market segments, and satisfy shareholder expectations of excellent financial returns. They focus on internal processes that will have the greatest impact on customer satisfaction and achieving an organisation's financial objectives. These measures include aspects of both the short-wave operations cycle and the long-wave innovation cycle. The internal measures for the balanced scorecard should stem from the business processes that have the greatest impact on customer satisfaction – factors that affect cycle time, quality, employee skills and productivity. Companies should also attempt to identify and measure their company's core competencies – what are their most important processes and how can they be measured:

- Reworks (e.g. number/percentage of off spec products)
- Percentage of customer orders not on time, on spec
- Response time (e.g. 24 hour repairs)
- On-time delivery (e.g. percentage of tests that meet the agreed-upon time)
- Accuracy of information (e.g. information systems capabilities)
- Margin opportunity analysis index (e.g. optimum production scheduling)
- Planned vs. actual throughputs
- Testing efficiency (e.g. average of all routine tests measured in hours)
- Ratio of approved to submitted orders
- Scrap/waste
- Speed of processing
- Measures of timeliness.

4.5.4 *Measures of innovation and learning*

The fourth perspective in the balanced scorecard is learning and growth. It identifies the infrastructure that the organisation must build to create long-term growth and improvement. Organisational learning and growth comes from three principle sources: people, systems, and organisational procedures. The financial, customer and internal business process objectives of the balanced scorecard typically will reveal large gaps between the existing capabilities of people, systems, and procedures and what will be required to achieve breakthrough performance. To close those gaps, businesses will have to invest in giving new skills to employees, enhancing information technology and systems, and aligning organisational procedures and routines. These objectives are articulated in the learning and growth perspective of the balanced scorecard. Employee-based measures include employee satisfaction, retention, training, and skills. Information systems can be measured by real-time availability of accurate, critical customer information to employees on the front-line of decision-making and actions. Organisational procedures can examine the alignment of employee incentives with overall organisational success factors. A company's ability to innovate, improve and learn ties directly to the company's value. That is, only through the ability to launch new products, create more value for customers, and improve operating efficiencies continually can a company penetrate new markets and increase revenues and margins, i.e. improve their shareholder value.

Measures of innovation and learning include:

- Percentage of revenues generated from products developed in the last *x* months.
- Number of patents.
- Patents per million dollars of R&D investment.
- Installation base of a particular new product or service.
- Overall satisfaction and commitment: employee survey-based measures, measures of turnover, measures of absenteeism.
- Drivers of overall satisfaction and commitment, including: survey-based measures, including employee perceptions of: confidence in leadership, recognition/reward, safety climate, teamwork, fair treatment, supervision, open communications.
- Drivers of performance – survey-based measures: rewards/incentives, perceived alignment of systems (reward, communication, performance management, succession, development, etc.) with strategy, skills training, climate for process improvement, goal clarity.
- Organisational learning: feedback systems, cross functional teamwork, supporting technology to enhance learning.
- Performance: output per employee (e.g. sales per employee, delivery per employee), quality of outputs.

NatWest UK has developed a balanced business scorecard using three key processes for translating strategy into action (FINPLUS, 1998). The strategic planning process takes a five year horizon, feeding to operational planning looking out two years, and this cascades back to performance measurement over a one year timeframe. This, in turn, loops back to the strategic planing process again. NatWest UK has also cascaded its balanced scorecard concept through the organisation, by creating regional and branch scorecards (Ashton, 1997).

Analog Devices, often thought to be the originator of the balanced scorecard, has been using it for more than a decade, particularly on leading indicators like new product development (Gendron, 1997). Their vice president of planning and development sees its purpose in simple terms:

Figure 4.7: Balanced scorecard example

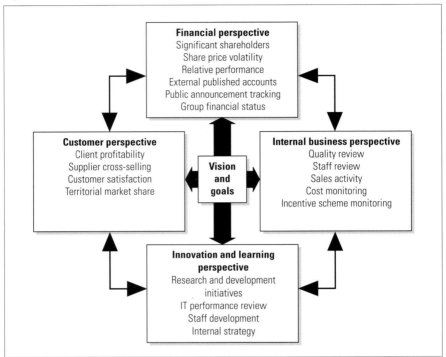

'Are we on-plan or off-plan? If all these new product measures are on-plan, that indicates that next year and the year after that will proba-bly be pretty good.'   (Gendron, 1997, p3).

Kaplan and Norton extend their thinking in proposing that the balanced scorecard is more than a new measurement system. Innovative companies use the balanced scorecard as the central, organising frame-work for their management processes. Companies can develop an initial scorecard with fairly narrow objectives. These objectives include gaining clarification, consensus, and focus on their strategy, as well as com-municating the strategy throughout the organisation. But they assert that the real power of the balanced scorecard comes when it is transformed from a measurement system to a management system. As more and more companies use the balanced scorecard, there is evidence that it can be used to:

- clarify and gain consensus about strategy;
- communicate strategy throughout the organisation;
- align departmental and personal goals to the strategy;
- link strategic objectives to long-term targets and annual budgets;
- identify and align strategic initiatives;
- perform periodic and systematic strategic reviews; and
- obtain feedback to learn about and improve strategy.

4.5.5 Implementing the balanced scorecard

Introducing a balanced scorecard means introducing a change in the company. Change is never easy and is especially difficult when it involves performance reporting and risks modifying the balance of power within the organisation. Research published in 1999, sponsored by the CIMA Research Foundation and undertaken by the University of Leeds, entitled *Shareholder and stakeholder approaches to strategic performance measurement using the balanced scorecard* focused on 500 UK organisations in both the private and public sector. It lists key points for managers involved in balanced scorecard design and implementation, as follows:

- *Link the scorecard and content to strategy* – Many scorecards are purely operational monitoring tools. Scorecards should be aligned with clear strategic objectives.
- *Link the scorecard to change initiatives and project evaluations* – Scorecards should be used explicitly to track the efforts of change programmes within the organisation.
- *Link the scorecard to stakeholder expectations* – In the private sector shareholder interests dominate. In the public sector there often exists a complex network of stakeholders. Scorecards need to reflect stakeholder expectations.
- *Understand the logic of value creation* – The scorecard should tell a comprehensive 'narrative' of how value is created in the organisation.
- *Understand end-user expectations* – Scorecard design requirements are different for executive teams than for operational departments. There is a limit to the benefits of aggregation of scorecard measures up organisational hierarchies.
- *Link to the external competitive environment* – There is a danger of making scorecards introspective. To be strategic, scorecards must be linked to monitoring discontinuities in external competitive environments.

- *Never believe that the numbers are more important than the issues* – Numerical values of reported performance indicators are less important than the agenda for debate that they generate.
- *Customise the scorecard design* – Best-practice organisations customise their scorecards. In some cases these become unrecognisable as scorecards.
- *Implementation: champion and consult* – Scorecard implementation needs a senior champion or sponsor. Success is dependent on wide consultation.
- *Day-to-day usage: encourage congruence* – The perceived benefits of scorecard usage should encourage congruent behaviour, which may be formalised in the linkage to appraisal and remuneration.

Thus, the balanced scorecard is more than just a tactical or an operational measurement system. Innovative companies are already using the scorecard as a strategic management system, to manage their strategy over the long run. The best balanced business scorecards are results-based. This begins with establishing or reaffirming the company's strategic imperatives – the results the organisation must attain. This step is followed by determining the drivers of the desired business results, and then the drivers of those, and so on until a complete model of the business is created.

Companies trying to implement a balanced scorecard can encounter difficulties along the following lines:

- Lack of top management support, poor communication, inadequate training and failure to secure widespread participation and support.
- Top management team cannot articulate a concise and shared view of the firm's strategy.
- Failure to tailor and adapt innovative practices to suit local circumstances.
- Developing and maintaining the balanced scorecard creates an excessive workload.
- Managers may be reluctant to give up some of their power base by contributing to the balanced scorecard.
- Pressure from competing reporting mechanisms.
- The cost and potentially disruptive effects of the balanced scorecard programme.
- Managers may be reluctant to let their operations become more visible and may see accountants who stray beyond their traditional domain of pure financial matters as intruders.

- Accountants may see the decentralisation of accounting information as the erosion of their power-base.

Research was carried out in Europe in 1996 by Professor Lewy of Amsterdam and Lex du Mee of KPMG using seven European companies as case studies, which resulted in findings known as the 'ten commandments of balanced scorecard implementation'. The objective was to try to understand the mixed success of the application of this simple, common sense concept of using a balanced set of performance indicators to run an organisation. The findings to be followed for successful implementation were concluded to be:

The DOs

- Use the scorecard as an implementation pad for strategic goals.
- Ensure that strategic goals are in place before the scorecard is implemented.
- Ensure that a top level (non-financial) sponsor backs the scorecard and that line managers are committed to the project.
- Implement a pilot before introducing the new scorecard.
- Carry out an 'entry review' for each business unit before implementing the scorecard.

The DON'Ts

- Use the scorecard to obtain extra top-down control.
- Attempt to standardise the project. The scorecard must be tailor-made.
- Underestimate the need for training and communication in using the scorecard.
- Seek complexity nor strive for perfection.
- Underestimate the extra administrative workload and costs of periodic scorecard reporting.

Evans *et al.* (1996) note that one method of ensuring that attention is given to critical strategic drivers of success is to form a broader set of performance measures into a balanced scorecard (in the SEM philosophy these being traditional performance measures extended to include SVM, benchmarking, and ABC/M). In Evans's view (1996), the scorecard technique recognises that companies need measures which look at the organisation from a variety of standpoints. They assert that the balanced scorecard provides the cornerstone of a strategic management system. One of the key

Figure 4.8: SEM and the balanced scorecard.

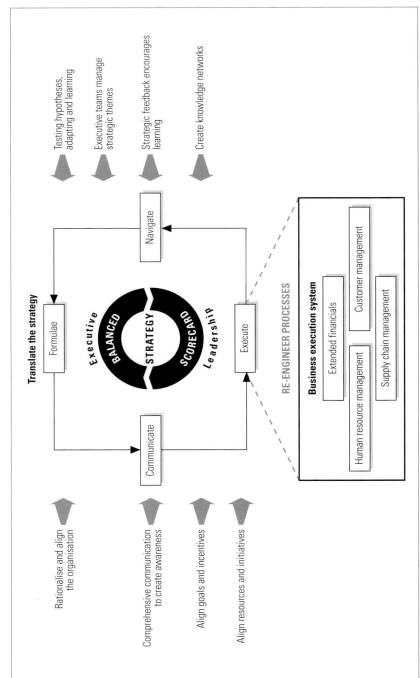

benefits of the approach is the ability to identify strategic conflicts and com-municate strategy within the organisation. Contemporary performance measurement systems also incorporate continuous improvement and emphasise the reporting of direct actionable measures at the operational level (Chenhall, 1999).

Kaplan and Norton (1996a, 1996b) also claim that the balanced scorecard fills the void that exists in most management systems, i.e. the lack of a systematic process to implement and obtain feedback about strategy. Management processes built around the scorecard enable the organisation to become aligned and focused on implementing the long-term strategy. They link the use of what starts out as a performance measurement system, i.e. the balanced scorecard, with the ongoing strategic management of the organisation in today's environment:

> 'Used in this way, the balanced scorecard becomes the foundation for managing information age organisations.'
>
> (Kaplan and Norton, 1996b, p.19)

Most of the SEM offerings in the market-place use the basic tenants of Kaplan and Norton to turn a balanced scorecard into an application that functions as the central nervous system for reporting and analysis. The challenge is for firms to combine the balanced scorecard framework with the support technology to deliver a performance measurement system which meets the unique needs of the firm's strategy.

4.6 Other accounting and management innovations

The last decade has been a time of many accounting and management innovations. In this section the link between ABC/M and innovations such as value chain analysis, life cycle costing, and target costing are discussed.

4.6.1 Activity-based budgeting

Budgets prepared using ABC concepts give superior results in terms of helping managers anticipate the effects of planned changes. ABC budget-ing can be used to simulate the effect of planned changes in activities. ABC budgeting links projected revenue to activities and activities to resources required thus producing a more realistic budget. Actual activity and resource drivers or budgeted activity and resource drivers may be used in the budgeting process. Budgeted activity and resource drivers will have planned efficiencies and planned reductions in surplus capacity built in. ABC budgeting greatly aids workload and resource requirement planning.

4.6.2 *Customer profitability analysis*

The cost of physical distribution and other marketing activities accounts for a significant proportion of total costs. The objective of market cost analysis is to provide relevant quantitative data that will assist marketing managers in making informed decisions regarding (a) product profitability, (b) pricing, and (c) adding or dropping a product line or territory, or sales channel. To achieve this objective it is necessary to be able to trace costs directly to product lines or territories and to establish a rational system of allocating non-traceable costs to the cost objective.

Distribution channel profitability is becoming increasingly important as products are sold through diverse channels, e.g. distributors, mega stores, direct mail. If the organisation serves a single channel, then channel profitability calculation is relatively straightforward. If the organisation is aligned by production, region, or facility location, then the calculation of profitability by channel is more difficult. Using ABC in this context costs products more accurately and also recognises that cost is driven not only by production activity but also by the customers served and the channels through which the product is offered. Not all costs can be related to products.

Examining the cost structure from this perspective allows management to understand cost differences related to one of these categories or related to interaction between the categories.

Figure 4.9: Channel profitability

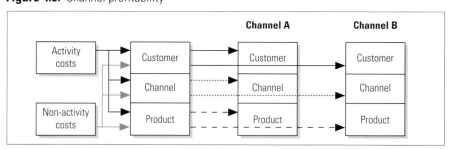

ABC can be used to determine how a company's customers consume its marketing, distribution and customer service resources. They said that customer profitability analysis is important because each £ of revenue does not contribute equally to profit. Profitability depends not only on the unit cost of the product but also on back end services (marketing, distribution and customer service).

4.6.3 *Supplier relationships*

ABC/M can play a major role in improving supplier relationships. The lowest cost supplier is not necessarily the cheapest in the long term. The total cost of making a batch of components available to production includes costs of purchase, ordering, paying, receiving, moving, storing, scrap, rework, obsolescence, scheduling, expediting and downtime. The supplier that provides materials that minimise the totality of these costs is the lowest cost supplier. The ABC model enables purchasing to estimate how much it is willing to pay a supplier so that the net gains can be shared between supplier and customer (lean supplier paradigm). ABC enables an informed trade-off among price, quality and responsiveness. ABC promotes long-term relationships with suppliers.

4.6.4 *Product design*

Turney noted that:

> 'Inappropriate cost systems can also thwart the benefits to be gained from world class design. Today's products are designed faster and brought to market in a fraction of the time it used to take.'

The Ford Motor Co estimated that 60–80 per cent of costs over a product's life cycle are locked in at the end of the product design phase and that 90–95 per cent are locked in by the time the design of the production process is complete. So design offers tremendous cost reduction opportunities.

Traditional unit-based cost systems, with their emphasis on overhead allocations based on direct labour promoted design strategies that minimised the direct labour content in the end product. This often resulted in increased costs overall. For example, the increased number of distinct parts included in the end product design results in increased procurement, storage and handling costs that outweigh the direct labour saving. Product engineer's design for manufacturability efforts, which aim to design products with fewer and more common parts, reduce the demands for product sustaining resources.

4.6.5 *Value chain analysis*

ABC links closely with value chain analysis (VCA) providing more accurate cost information at each level of the value chain. Managing costs requires a broad focus on what Porter calls the value chain – the linked set of value creating activities. The focus is *external* to the firm with each firm viewed in the context of the overall chain of value creating activities of which the firm is only a part, from basic raw material to end use consumers. Value added, on the other hand, is focused largely internal to the firm with each firm viewed in the context of its purchases, processes, functions, products and customers. The aim of value added is to maximise the difference (value added) between sales and purchases. The strategic insights yielded by VCA are superior to those offered by value added analysis. The value-added concept starts too late and ends too early when compared to VCA.

Porter noted that a business can develop a sustainable competitive advantage by following either a low cost strategy or a differentiation strategy. Whether or not a firm can develop and sustain cost leadership or differentiation depends on how it manages its value chain relative to those of its competitors. Competitive advantage ultimately derives from providing better customer value for equivalent cost or equivalent customer value for lower cost.

The value chain framework is a method for breaking down the chain into strategically relevant activities in order to understand the behaviour of costs and sources of differentiation. Gaining and sustaining a competitive advantage requires the firm to understand the entire value delivery system, not just the portion of the value chain in which it participates. Suppliers and distributors have profit margins that are important to identify in understanding a firm's cost or differentiation position, as end use customers pay for *all* the profit margins throughout the value chain.

VCA promotes interdependence along the value chain. It promotes mutually beneficial linkages backward to suppliers and forward to customers.

Insights offered by VCA:

- VCA is a first step in understanding how a firm is positioned in its industry. Building sustainable competitive advantage requires a knowledge of the full linked set of value-added activities of which the firm and its competitors are a part.
- Once a value chain is articulated, strategic decisions such as make vs. buy or forward vs. backward integration become clearer. Investments can be viewed from their impact on the overall chain and the firms place in it.
- VCA helps quantify buyer and supplier power.
- VCA highlights how a firm's product fits into its customer's value chain. It is readily apparent what percentage the firm's costs are of the customer's total costs. It encourages joint cost reductions.

4.6.6 *Life cycle costing*

Life cycle costing adds a new perspective to ABC programmes highlighting the interdependence of activities and their associated costs at all stages of product life cycles. Life cycle costing looks at products over their life cycle rather than just for one year. A product's life cycle encompasses initial research and development, proceeds through the product launch, growth in the market and ends with maturity, decline and abandonment. A life cycle perspective yields insights to product costs and profitability not available from viewing a single year. A product that is in a start-up phase may appear uncompetitive with its low volumes and high marketing costs while a mature product with its higher volumes will appear highly profitable.

A key to the success of life cycle costing is the accuracy of product life and costs. The basis for target costing is profitability over the lifetime of the product.

4.7 Future directions for finance

A quick scan of management accounting literature shows that there are many issues in respect of performance measurement and management accounting and control systems under review. Indeed, there is now so much advice available that the range of new approaches is building up to the point of some confusion. Management accountants and the techniques they use have long been under attack for failing to adapt to the new competitive environment of global competition, decentralisation, and the rise of knowledge-based assets. The new environment demands more relevant cost and performance information on the organisation's activities, processes, products, services, and customers.

Change inevitably brings uncertainty. Changes in management accounting and control systems and practice bring uncertainty for finance professionals and for finance functions in general. Managers and staff working in these roles will need to adapt to the new environment or face a growing lack of relevance in their organisations. Kaplan (1995) suggests that finance professionals should:

- become part of the value-added team of the organisation;
- participate in the formulation and implementation of strategy;
- translate strategic intent and capabilities into operational and managerial measures; and

- move away from being scorekeepers of the past and become the designers of the organisation's critical management information systems.

One response is to maintain the status quo by claiming that the management accountant has a valuable role to play and to try to make that role even more critical to the firm. The alternate response is to take management accounting to the user and to actively support the cost management process. This involves decentralising much of the management accounting function to the users, resulting in a fall in the need for management accountants, while the need for management accounting will rise.

Management accountants face competition from other groups who, through widespread access to data, can provide and acquire information without the use of management accountants. Yet the diffusion of technology supporting decision-making in different forms, makes it even more crucial that information be used properly. As the management accountant has considerable competitive advantage in the analysis of data and the building and interpretation of financial models, it is essential to actually get involved in the design and implementation of the new technology.

Phillips (1996) expands this by looking at the finance function as a whole. He notes that the two main drivers for change in the finance function are improved information technology and the pace of business change. He summarises the main changes facing finance functions in Table 4.2.

For management accountants to rise to full business partnership, they need to change their traditional internal and historical focus. While maintaining their financial capabilities, management accountants must build new requisite skills, such as broadened business knowledge, expert analytic capability, and team building and partnership expertise.

Table 4.2: Changes in the finance function

	Finance function today is characterised by:	In the future the function will be:
Role	Professional advisors	Specialist team members
	Detached from the business	Involved in/understanding the business
	Stewards	Business partners
	Tactical	Strategic
People	Gurus	A learning organisation
	Hard skills/old skills	Soft skills/new skills
Organisation	Function	Matrix
	Silo	Embedded
	Multi-function	Split function
	Hierarchical	Flat
Services	Retention of all activities	Outsourcing specialist activities
	Historically focused	Future viewing
	Internally driven	Customer-facing
	Inflexible	Flexible
	Financial information	Balanced scorecard
	Routine	Exception/project based
	Internally focused management attention	Outwardly focused and focused on change
IT	Technology resistant	Exploiting technology
	Automating today's processes	Automating re-engineered processes
	Paper based	Utilising electronic documents
	A spreadsheet culture	Integrated, automated information provision

Strategic enterprise management technologies   **5**

From MIS to ERP and beyond

5.1 Introduction

Many firms that installed computers during the 1970s and 1980s failed either to integrate these financial and other resource management related transaction-processing systems with their business strategy, or to keep abreast of technological changes. Developed in an age of mainframe programing languages, the systems were troublesome to document, costly to maintain and difficult to change as business conditions evolved. This resulted in many finance systems and processes becoming stand alone and requiring very large amounts of expensive manual intervention.

A survey conducted by Tate Bramald Consultancy (1996) for CIMA/JBA revealed that 83 per cent of UK management accountants surveyed used spreadsheets to produce their management accounts, compared to 13 per cent who used enterprise-wide systems. These findings are confirmed by a report produced by Bournemouth University for IBM. This research found that more than 75 per cent of finance professionals believe that their personal computer (PC) is essential for business, but only 45 per cent take full advantage of the networked collaborative applications available: the rest use their PCs merely to compile spreadsheets and other basic financial documents. Highly labour-intensive re-keying of data from other source systems to spreadsheets for reporting is still the norm for many accountants.

5.2 From traditional ERP to SEM

Earlier generations of systems (such as MRP and MRP II) were designed within the limits of available technology for that time. In the late 1970s, when MRP II was first emerging, there were no relational databases, computer memories were measured in kilobytes, and processor speeds were still crossing the bridge between milliseconds and microseconds. Developers were unable to build systems that bridged multiple sites and ultimately converged for planning and control purposes. The advent of better technology allowed vendors to develop complex systems that were truly enterprise wide, and consequently, a new name, enterprise resource planning (ERP), was coined for these systems.

In the past, numerous disparate systems were contained within manufacturing, distribution, finance, and sales. Taking information from every function, ERP systems are a tool that assists employees and managers to plan, monitor and control the entire business. A modern ERP system enhances a firm's ability to accurately schedule production, fully utilise capacity, reduce inventory, and meet promised shipping dates. In simplest terms, enterprise systems use database technology and a single interface to control all the information related to a company's business, including customer, product, employee, and financial data. The term 'enterprise resource planning' was coined to reflect the fact that these computerised systems have evolved well beyond their origins as inventory transaction and cost accounting systems. The software has become the means to support and speed the entire order-fulfilment process and to automate and integrate both business and production process management. By recording all transactions (e.g. receipt of inventory, issue of a work order, etc.), the ERP system tracks resources, such as materials and labour, used in financial, manufacturing and distribution management.

An ERP system is a software system that allows a company to automate and integrate its business processes, to share common data and processes across the enterprise and to generate and share information in a real-time environment. Davenport argues that:

'an enterprise system streamlines a company's data flows and provides management with direct access to a wealth of real-time operating information.'

He suggests that:

'A good enterprise system is a technological tour de force. At its core is a single comprehensive database. The database collects data and then feeds data into modular applications supporting virtually all of a company's business activities – across functions, across business units, across the world. When new information is entered in one place, related information is automatically updated.'

A key feature of ERP software is that it is process oriented, not task oriented. It forces standardisation of codes, processes and hierarchy and eliminates cross-system reconciliations. It increases information flow, promotes workflow automation and provides a cohesive internal environment. These processes and data are integrated across the above modules in the one enterprise-wide system (see Figure 5.1).

If implemented correctly, the system provides quality data that is consistent, reliable and timely, and is available throughout the organisation in order to effectively manage the business. The premise of ERP is to enable a consolidation and unification of the various processes required by an organisation to meet its strategic business objectives. ERP's goal is to integrate a broad range of disparate technologies, along with the processes they support, into a common denominator of overall functionality. Contemporary ERP systems permit organisations to manage resources across the enterprise and enable the integration of sales management, component procurement, inventory management, manufacturing control, project management, distribution, transportation, finance and other functions.

At the heart of the ERP concept is an extensive library of more than 1000 predefined business processes spanning each functional software requirement (see Table 5.1). These processes may be selected from the ERP library and included within installed ERP applications, tailoring the application solution to suit the user's exact requirements. New business processes and technologies become available regularly. ERP systems are multi-site, multi-company, multi-currency, functional information systems running over distributed client/server environments. The power of ERP software lies in real-time integration, linking a company's business processes and applications, and supporting immediate responses to change throughout the organisation on a departmental, divisional or global scale. The international natures of ERP products extends to every aspect of the applications, such as the support of multiple currencies simultaneously and the automatic handling of country-specific import/export, tax, legal and language requirements.

An effective ERP architecture will typically have the following characteristics:

- *Flexibility:* An ERP system should be flexible to respond to the changing needs of an enterprise. It should be capable of embracing new technologies, such as mobile computing and the Internet.

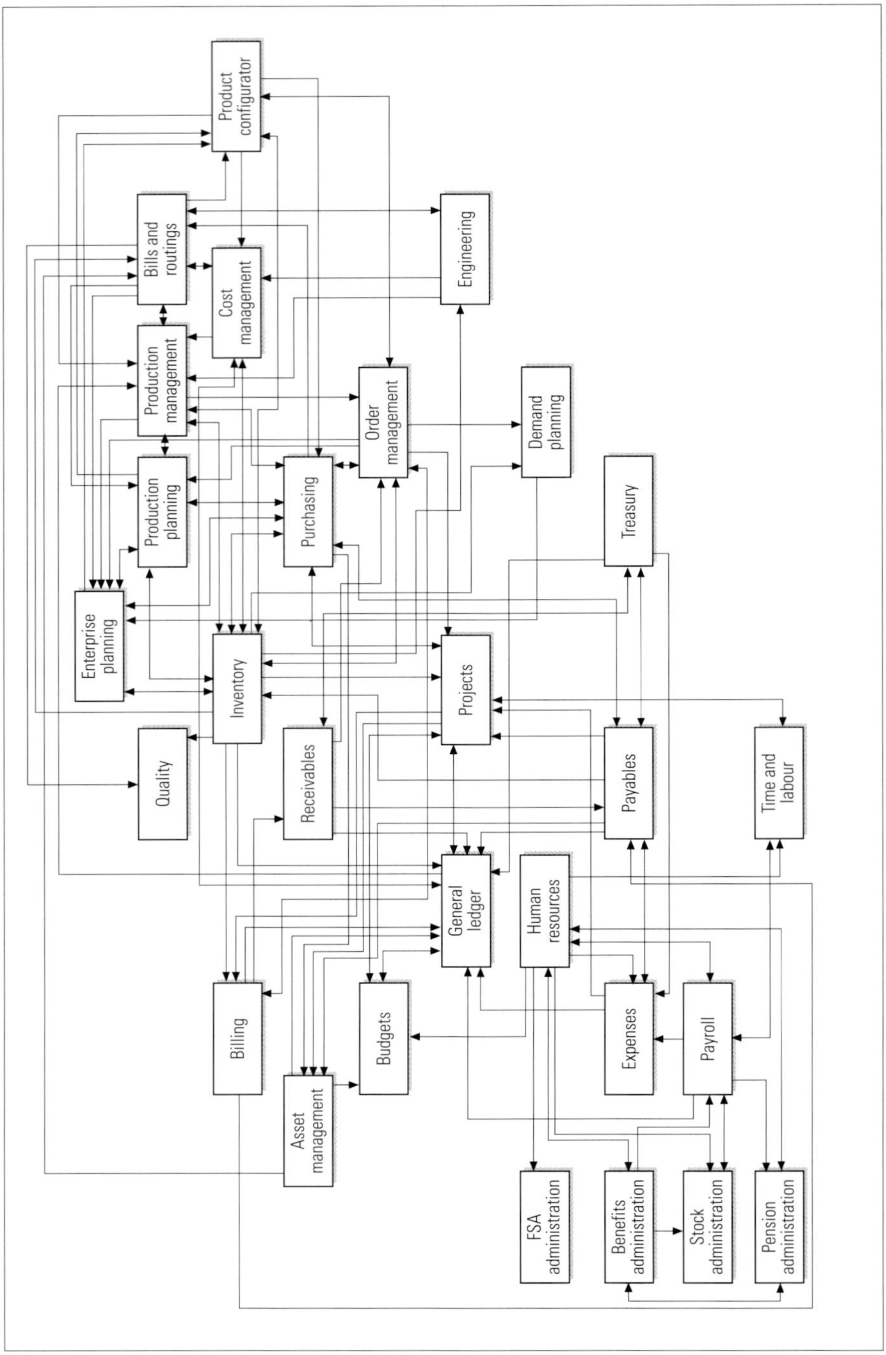

Figure 5.1: The reach and range of ERP systems across the business processes. © J.D. Edwards & Company, used by permission.

Table 5.1: JD Edwards ERP systems functionality. © J.D. Edwards & Company, used by permission

Foundation Suite	**Project Management Suite**
Back Office	Procurement
CASE Foundation	Inventory Management
Environment/Toolkit	Equipment Management
Financial Analysis Spreadsheet Tool and	Job Cost
Report Writer	Work Order Management
WorldVision GUI	Subcontract Management
Electronic Burst & Bind	Change Management
Financial Suite	Contract Management
General Accounting	Contract Billing
Accounts Payable	Service Billing
Accounts Receivable	Property Management
Fixed Assets	**Energy and Chemical Suite**
Financial Modeling and Budgeting	Agreement Management
Multi-Currency Processing	Advanced Stock Valuation
Cash Basis Accounting	Sales Order Management
Time Accounting	Bulk Stock Management
Canadian Payroll	Load and Delivery Management
Logistics/Distribution Suite	**Payroll Suite**
Forecasting	Payroll
Requirements Planning	Time Accounting
Enterprise Facilities Planning	**Human Resources Suite**
Sales Order Management	Human Resources
Advanced Pricing	**Customer Service Management Suite**
Procurement	Customer Service Management
Work Order Management	**Government, Education, and Not-for-Profit**
Inventory Management	**Solutions**
Bulk Stock Management	Financial Administration and Reporting
Quality Management	Budget Administration
Advanced Warehouse Management	Fund and Encumbrance Accounting
Equipment Management	Grant and Endowment Management
Transportation Management	Purchasing and Material Management
Job Cost	Warehousing and Central Stores Management
Service Billing	Human Resources Management
Services Suite	Service and Work Order Management
Contract Billing	Capital Project and Construction Management
Subcontract Management	Contract Management
Change Management	Plant, Equipment, and Fleet Maintenance
Property Management	**Utility and Energy Solutions**
Manufacturing Suite	Customer Information System
Configuration Management	Human Resources Management
Cost Management	Work Management
Product Data Management	Regulatory Reporting
Capacity Planning	Supply Chain Management
Shop Floor Management	Project Management
Advanced Maintenance Management	Enterprise Maintenance Management

- *Modular and open:* An ERP system has to have an open system architecture. This means that any module can be interfaced or detached whenever required without affecting the other modules. In addition, an ERP system should be capable of integrating with best of breed applications in areas such as customer relationship management (CRM), data mining and simulation.
- *Comprehensive:* It should be able to support a variety of organisational functions and must be suitable for a wide range of business organisations. While many early ERP systems had their origins in manufacturing and operations, a mature ERP system will offer functionality across the value chain from in bound logistics to customer facing processes
- *Beyond the company:* It should not be confined to the organisational boundaries, rather it should support the on-line connectivity to the other business entities of the organisation.
- *Best business practices:* It must have a collection of the best business processes applicable worldwide.

As ERP systems have evolved, functionality has been introduced to support the specific needs of vertical industry segments, such as consumer packaged goods or automotive manufacturers, as well as special operations such as demand management, an essential feature for better management of supply chains. ERP systems have begun to incorporate functionality for customer interaction and managing relationships with suppliers and vendors, making the system less inward looking. Figure 5.2 shows the typical functionality found in an ERP system implemented in the automotive sector. The system supports the complete range of processes including those which are unique to the automotive sector.

Vendors are working hard to make ERP more useable for small- to mid-sized manufacturers, particularly in the area of implementations, which can cost as much as five times the software licenses. Other value-added aspects of the newest systems include product configuration, electronic data interchange, field service modules, and Internet capabilities that extend system access to more users. ERP is also a means for business process re-engineering, increasing flexibility and responsiveness by breaking down barriers between functional departments and reducing duplication of efforts.

The consistency of ERP system data provides improved information for analysis and a seamless reconciliation from the general ledger to sub

Figure 5.2: The architecture of ERP – an example from the automotive industry.

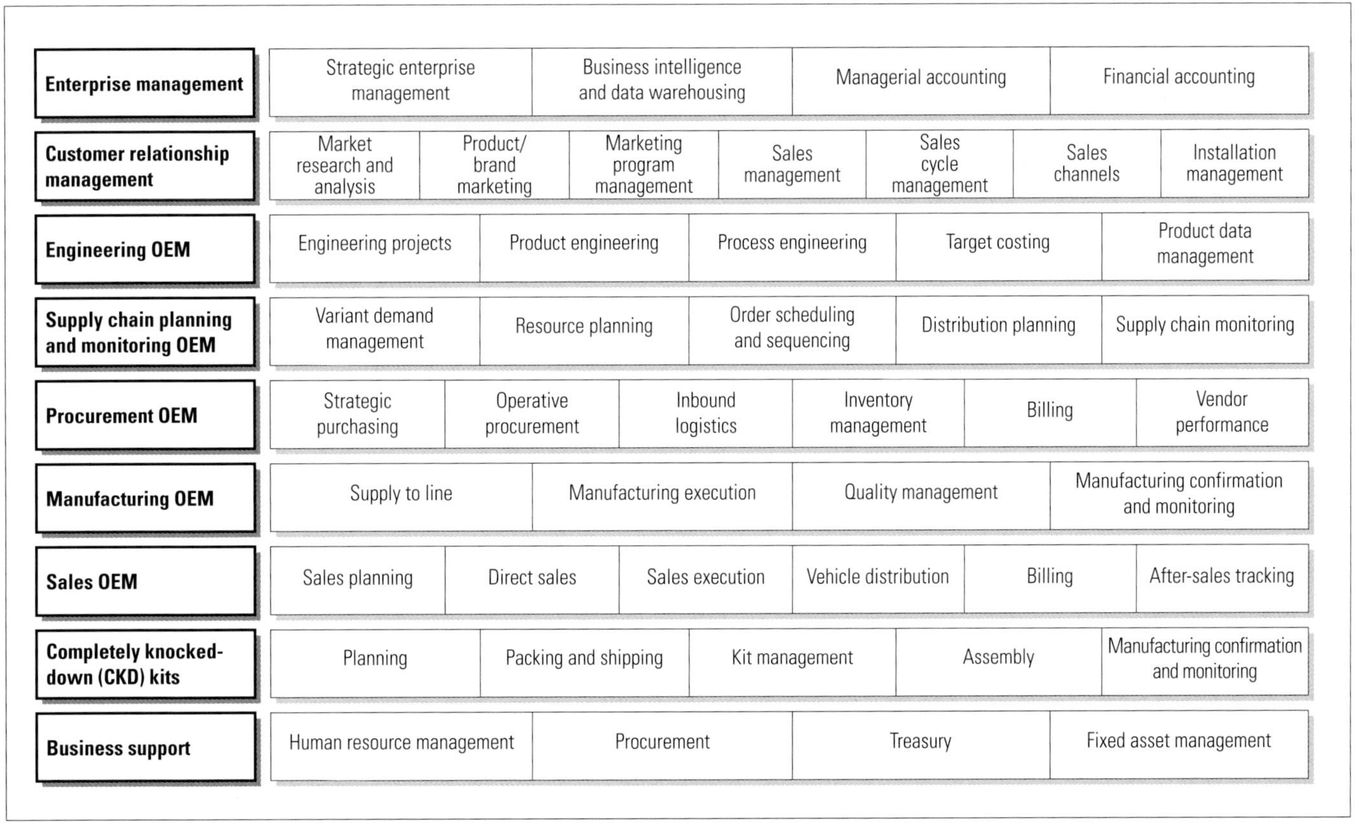

Enterprise management	Strategic enterprise management		Business intelligence and data warehousing	Managerial accounting		Financial accounting
Customer relationship management	Market research and analysis	Product/brand marketing	Marketing program management	Sales management	Sales cycle management	Sales channels	Installation management
Engineering OEM	Engineering projects	Product engineering	Process engineering	Target costing		Product data management
Supply chain planning and monitoring OEM	Variant demand management	Resource planning	Order scheduling and sequencing	Distribution planning		Supply chain monitoring
Procurement OEM	Strategic purchasing	Operative procurement	Inbound logistics	Inventory management	Billing	Vendor performance
Manufacturing OEM	Supply to line	Manufacturing execution		Quality management		Manufacturing confirmation and monitoring
Sales OEM	Sales planning	Direct sales	Sales execution	Vehicle distribution	Billing	After-sales tracking
Completely knocked-down (CKD) kits	Planning	Packing and shipping	Kit management	Assembly		Manufacturing confirmation and monitoring
Business support	Human resource management	Procurement		Treasury		Fixed asset management

© SAP AG.

ledgers. The data is updated in real time throughout the month. With innate ERP integration, a physical transaction cannot be booked without the resulting financial effect being shown. This visibility of activities across finance and operations gives operational managers the ability to better understand the effects of their decisions. With ERP systems the company's financial organisation is better equipped to:

- provide decision support to corporate leadership;
- create strategic performance measures; and
- engage in strategic cost management.

A number of lessons have emerged from experiences with ERP systems:

1. Organisations need to recognise that ERP systems are an established part of the IT/IS infrastructure and will provide the transaction processing backbone for many years to come. In particular ERP systems will be a key enabling technology in the bid to embrace and exploit the opportunities of e-business.

2. The functionality of ERP systems will continue to expand and will embrace such areas as CRM, ABM, SEM and other areas. The future focus of ERP will shift from helping firms do things right to helping firms do the right things.

3. The level of investment required to effectively deploy ERP systems will continue to grow. The next five years will see a significant ERP effort in the areas of enterprise application integration arising from e-business initiatives and other changes. The existing ERP infrastructure will also need to be maintained and in some cases renewed. All of this will require a substantial commitment of resources from organisations. Firms which continue to view ERP systems in cost avoidance terms will find it increasingly hard to justify their ERP investments. As the total cost of ownership increases those instrumental in deploying ERP will have to show a real contribution to shareholder value.

4. The finance function will be expected to play a key role in benefits realisation from the ERP investment. CFOs and their support staffs, including management accountants, will be expected to measure and drive out the benefits identified in the original business case for ERP. Accordingly finance will have to move to centre stage in leveraging the investment made to date.

5. Systems integration issues will continue to consume large amounts of resources. As firms continue to partner, merge and acquire, the requirement to integrate diverse systems across the organisation and its value chain will increase. The emergence of business to business (b2b) trading hubs and e-business will re-open the systems integration problems which ERP originally set out to solve in the early 1990s.

6. The future focus of ERP will be the value chain and, in particular. the ensuring that the firm does not lose opportunities for value creation to other players in the broader supply chain. In this regard ERP systems will play an important role in projecting the firm's market power across the supply chain.

5.3 The technological blueprint of SEM

Traditional ERP systems were designed to aggregate data and ultimately to help companies achieve greater efficiency. These new generation SEM systems are designed to take ERP systems to the next level: to make data multidimensional and meaningful and thus to help organisations become effective through strategic analysis and simulation.

Thus, it is an evolved state or next generation solution to traditional ERP systems. SEM aims to extend the principles of ERP vertically to support high level value management processes, such as strategic planning, risk management and value communication. This will be achieved through the linking of ERP with business intelligence tools such as data mining, on-line analytical processing engines, desktop analysis and data visualisation software. It will allow for a two-way flow of information, for example, corporate strategists can monitor performance continuously using feed back from the business execution systems, and changes to strategy can be driven down to operational level through new targets and key performance indicators.

All of the main vendors have configured their offerings along similar dimensions, for example SAP in their offering aim to provide managers with business performance monitoring, consolidation and data warehousing/business intelligence capabilities. In conjunction with this information-management functionality they also aim to include techniques such as shareholder value management, balanced scorecards, performance management, benchmarking and ABC/M. It has been argued that many of the applications and tools offered by these new systems offer nothing essentially new and simply mirror the functionality that was previously offered in such technologies as decision support systems, executive information sys-

Figure 5.3: The technical nature of SEM

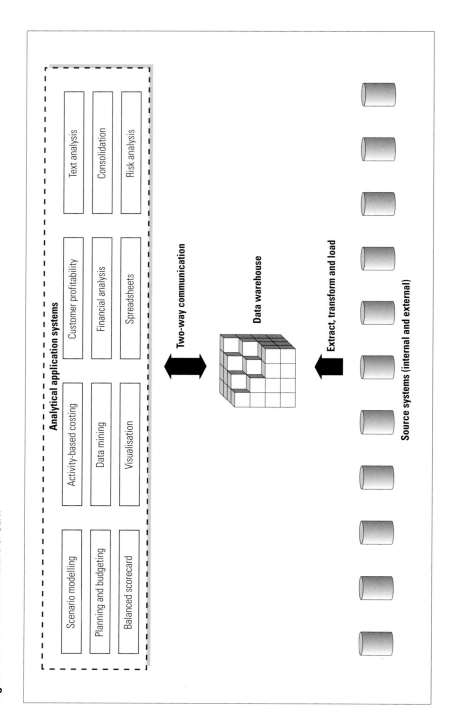

tems or previous data warehousing technologies. However, it is the processes and techniques that the adoption of these new systems instil into organisations that will possibly be the greatest asset they provide.

SEM brings together a number of technologies which are designed to support managers and provide business intelligence and an environment for decision-making through an accessible source of consistent information, i.e. a data warehouse and a suite of flexible systems for consolidation, analysis, planning and communication, data mining software, OLAP, and data visualisation software. The ultimate aim of the SEM technologies is to facilitate an environment, which has decision support and business intelligence at its core.

The basic tenets of the SEM technological blueprint can be explained as follows: ERP and the SEM technologies and techniques deliver operational, internal, external, financial and non-financial data to the data warehouse – ensuring consistent, maintainable, and sustainable information from across the organisation. Then sophisticated business intelligence analytic applications, easy to use desktop reporting tools, and preconfigured analysis templates deliver the information to the end user. The data warehouse provides the tremendous advantage of having all relevant information in a central location.

The diverse range of information needed to support an enterprise requires the gathering of data from outside of the traditional arena of the finance and logistics systems. To be competitive a data warehouse must be able to access these systems from across a range of vendors.

To access existing ERP systems within an organisation the simplest option is to align the business warehouse vendor with that of the existing ERP system vendor. With the system's diversity within individual companies, (often resulting from mergers and takeovers), this is not always possible. To address this issue the major players utilise different technologies to enable the extraction, transformation and loading of data into the warehouse from a variety of sources.

PeopleSoft's Enterprise Warehouse relies on third party tools with built-in capability to 'read' non-PeopleSoft database structures. Similarly Oracle's 'transparent gateway' allows access to non-Oracle databases as if they were Oracle, enabling the use of standard oracle query tools to extract data. Figure 5.4 illustrates Oracle's toolkit and integration to third party products. This is typical of the approach for all major ERP vendors.

The SEM business intelligence (BI) analytic applications take the data in the data warehouse a step further, turning the raw data into strategic information for analysis and reporting. Using these analytic applications, data from the data warehouse is transferred based on advanced business theories, best-practices, rules, and workflows determined by the individual organisation (Myrtveit, 2001). With its robust web-based reporting and intuitive web inter-face, SEM is designed to transcend the client/server model of distributed data and present a new model: wide access to data and to what the data means. SEM is designed to allow organisations to distribute meaningful data analy-sis throughout the enterprise, not just to managers or specialists.

Expressly the areas under review in this section are SEM data ware-housing and the associated data warehousing technologies and techniques (OLAP, extraction, transformation and loading (ETL), Metadata Management, Data Marts, InfoSources, and InfoCubes), SEM data mining, and SEM data visualisation (highlighted within Figure 5.4).

Figure 5.4: SEM architecture highlighting the SEM BI analytic applications

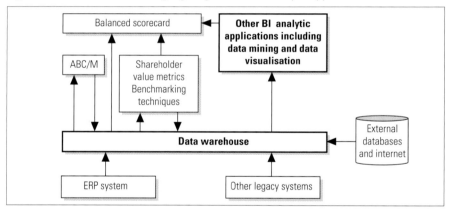

5.4 Strategic enterprise management and data warehousing

Most of the data required to produce the information needed by executives is locked away or scattered, available redundantly but out of sync, or a combination of these. Data warehousing has the potential to provide a solution to these data access and information analysis problems.

A data warehouse is a means of supporting management decision-making. It is intended to be used for analysis and strategic decision-making. The primary goal of data warehousing is to create the ability for any user to access quality integrated enterprise data easily. Data is made available from the data warehouse in a consistent form to support business decision-making rather than transaction processing. Data warehousing has evolved from a way to do complex queries into a tool to satisfy business managers needs not just for complex queries but for a general facility to get quick, accurate and insightful information.

Today for many organisations, the data warehouse is the foundation of decision support activities. Because there is a single integrated source of data in the data warehouse and because the data are accessible, the job of the business analyst is immeasurably easier than in the classical environment. With a data warehouse in place, the finance professional can be in a proactive position rather than a reactive position. The requirements of the finance function that are supported by the data warehouse include:

● the need for quick information;
● the need of management (executive to front-line) to change their mind;
● their need to look at data over a spectrum of time; and
● their need to drill down.

The characteristics of a data warehouse as defined by Inmon (1995) are described below:

● *Subject-oriented*: The database is subject oriented because of a shift from application-oriented data, to decision-support data.
● *Integrated*: The database is integrated because of the consolidation of application-oriented data from different legacy systems. This is the most important characteristic.
● *Time-variant*: The database is time-variant because of the distinction between operational and informational data.
● *Non-volatile*: New data is always appended to the database rather than replaced. The database continually absorbs new data integrating it with the previous data (Hackathorn, 1995).

In a 1996 study, Sakaguchi and Frolick undertook a comprehensive literature review of over 450 data warehousing articles. In this study the authors explicitly addressed the organisational advantages and disadvantages of deploying data warehousing. Their findings are summarised in Table 5.2.

Table 5.2: The advantages of data warehousing

1.	Simplicity. The data warehouse provides a single image of the business reality by integrating various data. They allow existing legacy systems to continue in operation, consolidate inconsistent data from various legacy systems into one coherent set, and reap benefits from vital information about current operations.
2.	Better quality data and improved productivity, through improved consistency, accuracy and documentation.
3.	Fast access. The necessary data is in one place.
4.	Easy to use. It is focused on subjects which are targeted to users.
5.	Separate decision support operation from production operation. Allows users the capability to navigate large organisational databases in an ad-hoc, interactive way without impacting mission critical operational systems.
6.	Gives competitive advantage

Source: Sakaguchi and Frolick (1997)

The data warehouse approach is necessary to successfully deploy SEM financial and analytic application capabilities on top of an existing ERP system. There are five reasons for this:

1. Data in the ERP is stored in normalised tables which may number, for example in the case of SAP, in excess of 9000 tables. This makes it difficult to extract the precise data required.
2. In order to get information out of the ERP system a multitude of small unit joins are required. This results in a very high processing overhead. Another issue arising from this is that data cannot then be easily presented to users in a structure which is meaningful to them.
3. Table and column names may not be easily recognisable. This is particularly evident in the SAP ERP offering as the tables are based on German abbreviations and mnemonics.
4. Most ERP systems use a proprietary internal storage format. For example, a cost centre hierarchy may be used resulting in poor cost code identification.
5. ERP systems cannot accommodate data from other sources.

Figure 5.5: The need for the data warehouse

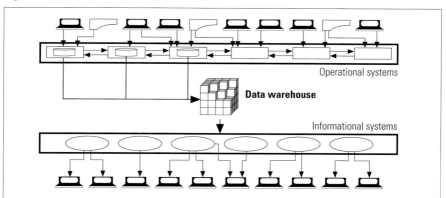

The data warehousing function is the result of the simple but significant observation that the systems used on a daily basis to run a business, operational systems (ERP), are fundamentally different from those used to plan and develop future businesses. These latter are referred to as informational systems. Operational data is organised around functional organisations within a business. Functionally oriented data is used to satisfy the immediate functional processing requirements of the business user; such a functional orientation is fine for operational data relevant to that area of the business. The differences between operational and informational systems are:

- *Operational systems – the business applications:* those business applications that operationally 'run' the business on a daily, weekly, monthly, etc., basis. When they cease to run, the business literally stops operating.
- *Informational systems – the 'about the business' applications:* those applications that analyse the business. They aid both in interpreting what has occurred and deciding prudent actions for the future. When they cease to run, there is no immediate, obvious business failure but their utility is critical to the long-term competitiveness of the enterprise. Data warehousing embraces these types of applications and it is this functionality that SEM aims to contribute to traditional ERP systems (see Figure 5.5).

Operational and informational data is also very important in the context of SEM data warehousing, as both reside within the SEM warehouse. All SEM systems currently available offer the functionality to cater for both operational and informational data storage.

5.4.1 Summarised data

Lightly summarised data are the hallmark of a SEM warehouse. All enterprise elements (department, region, function, etc.) do not have the same information requirements, so effective SEM warehouse design provides for customised, lightly summarised data for every enterprise element. An enterprise element may have access to both detailed and summarised data, but there will be much less than the total stored in current detail.

Highly summarised data can come from either the lightly summarised data used by enterprise elements or from current detail. Data volume at this level is much less than other levels and represents an eclectic collection supporting a wide variety of needs and interests. In addition to access to highly summarised data, all levels of management also have the capability of accessing increasing levels of detail through a 'drill down' process.

5.4.2 Current detail

The heart of a SEM warehouse is its current detail, where the bulk of data resides. Current detail comes directly from operational systems and may be stored as raw data or as aggregations of raw data. Current detail, organised by subject area, represents the entire enterprise, rather than a given application. Current detail is the lowest level of data granularity in the SEM warehouse.

5.4.3 Archives

SEM warehouse archives contain old data (normally over two years old) of significant, continuing interest and value to the enterprise. There is usually a massive amount of data stored in the SEM warehouse archives, with a low incidence of access. Archive data are most often used for forecasting and trend analysis. Although archive data may be stored with the same level of granularity as current detail, it is more likely that archive data are aggregated as they are archived.

Table 5.3: SEM software tools for data analysis

OLAP (On-line analytical processing)

A method of viewing data multidimensionally, is defined by OLAP Council as 'a category of software technology that enables analysts, managers and executives to gain insight into data through fast, consistent, interactive access to a wide variety of possible views of information that has been transformed from raw data to reflect the real dimensionality of the enterprise as understood by the user'. It largely depends on users to extract explanations from the data. Other tools in this family include ROLAP (Rational On-line Analytical Processing), DOLAP (Desktop On-line Analytical Processing) and MOLAP (Multidimensional On-line Analytical Processing).

Query tools

Facilitate ad-hoc query. They are used by non-programers to access the database using plain English.

Statistical tools

Examples SAS and SPSS.

Data visualisation

Shipped with the SEM product, data visualisation tools provide a pictorial representation of data which helps improve comprehension of complex business data.

Desktop presentation

Provides simple interface for users. A newly emerging presentation technology is the use of the world wide web.

Reporting software

Increases the ease of report creation.

5.5 SEM and data analysis

In order to achieve effective decision-making, managers demand data analysis applications, which are placed on top of their data warehousing solutions, to be versatile in providing different views of the information. Besides carrying out the tasks of analysing data, software is also needed to present the information to managers in the way they understand and can use. Data analysis software includes intelligent agents, OLAP, query tools, and statistical tools, and the software responsible for information present-ation includes data visualisation, desktop presentation, and reporting soft-ware, which is summarised in Table 5.3.

Many of these technologies have been in use for more than a decade in specialised analysis tools that work with relatively small volumes of data. SEM data analysis software products are the first package software tools to provide this combined functionality and are often the integration of products from vendors from various areas, including software engineering, statistics and graphics presentation.

On-line analytical processing (OLAP) is a type of software technology that enables analysts, managers, and executives to gain insight into data through fast, consistent, interactive access to a wide variety of possible views of information that has been transformed from raw data to reflect the real dimensionality of the enterprise as understood by the user. In other words, OLAP is a set of functionalities that can facilitate multidimensional analysis and manipulate aggregated data into various categories.

Data warehousing has traditionally focused on relational technology. While suited to managing transactions and storing large amounts of data, relational databases are typically unable to handle ad-hoc, speed of thought analytical querying for large user communities. OLAP technology, however, provides the scalability, performance and analytic capabilities necessary to support sophisticated, calculation intensive queries for large user (SEM) populations. For these reasons, relational and OLAP technologies are combined for maximum benefits within the SEM environment.

With the support of OLAP for multidimensional analysis, users can synthesise enterprise information through comparative customised viewing as well as an analysis of historical and projected data. Therefore, OLAP is an important addition within the SEM data warehouse architecture. With the increasing understanding of the capabilities of DSS processing and the growing volume of data, there is an increasing need for more sophisticated techniques to facilitate the use of the data warehouse.

The main characteristics of SEM OLAP products include:

- *Fast on-line access*. SEM OLAP processing is much more flexible than organisationally structured processing. In addition, the OLAP environment has a limited history at the same level of detail. Besides, with OLAP tools, users do not need to view the data in standard report formats, but rather in grids or cross-tabs so that they can quickly look at the data from different perspectives.
- *Strong analysis and deriving capability*. Departmentally structured data in the SEM OLAP environment are usually organised into predefined categories to facilitate the informational requirements of a

specific department, although they originate from the organisationally structured level of the data warehouse. For example, a department may want a particular metric that is pre-computed, and the results are stored in its OLAP environment. A similar metric may be stored at the organisationally structured level, but the department wants to compare its department-specific calculation to the organisation-standard one.

- *Strong query organising capability*. SEM OLAP involves an interactive querying of the data. Therefore, users can follow a train of thought by looking at information at one aggregation level, such as a sales region, and then drilling down into successively more detailed information, such as county, city, and store.
- *Aggregate capability*. SEM OLAP supports departmental customisation due to its strong aggregate capability. For example, the accounting department may summarise its data in one way while the finance department summarises its data in another. OLAP allows the use of different approaches for different data applications, calculations, and organisations.

The most widely used OLAP software in the finance area is Hyperion Essbase, which is a client/server OLAP technology. It is used in conjunction with Hyperion Integration server which facilitates rapid deployment of OLAP applications from rational sources, and provides the metadata linkage to drill down to warehouse data.

5.6 SEM and data mining

Although a mixture of statistical techniques and file management tools once sufficed for digging through mounds of corporate data, the size of modern data warehouses, the mission critical nature of the data, and the speed at which analysis needs to be made, now call for a new approach. Data mining is seen by many organisations as the approach in question. Data mining is essentially the process of selecting, exploring and modelling large amounts of data to uncover previously unknown patterns for business advantage. Data mining can be seen as an attempt to identify relationships between variables in data warehouses in order to assist decision-making. Data mining, by its simplest definition, automates the detection of relevant patterns in a database.

Data mining applications utilise the information stored in the warehouse to generate business-oriented, end-user-customised information. This synergy created between data warehousing and data mining allows goal-oriented decision-makers to leverage their massive data assets, thereby improving the effectiveness and quality of their decisions. Four elements of data in the data warehouse enhance the data mining process:

1. *Detailed and summarised data* – detailed data is necessary for uncovering patterns and trends, and summarised data allows end users to build on the findings of others and to avoid repetitive work.
2. *Integrated data* – well structured and consistent data makes the mining easier.
3. *Historical data* – historical data is crucial for businesses to understand their seasonality and business cycles.
4. *Metadata* – metadata provides the context of data and serves as a roadmap for end users in data mining.

Thus data mining is a powerful technology with great potential to help companies focus on the most important information in their data warehouses. Data mining tools can predict future trends and behaviours which in turn allow businesses to make proactive, knowledge-driven decisions. The automated analyses offered by data mining moves beyond the analysis of past events provided by traditional decision support systems and allows firms to answer business questions that were traditionally too time consuming to resolve.

There is a wide variety of features that are commonly found in data mining applications and different types of data mining renders different types of information, as can be seen in Table 5.4.

A range of conventional statistical methods can be applied such as cluster analysis, discriminant analysis, multiple regression, logic regression and time series forecasting. Multiple regression, for example, can be used to uncover a pattern of dependencies between multiple predictor fields and an outcome field, given a dependency does indeed exist. The most commonly used techniques in data mining are:

●   *Decision trees:* Decision trees illustrate dependencies between data in the form of branches of a decision tree. The user can easily see how an outcome field changes with the different values of the predictor fields. Tree-based models are good at selecting important predictor fields and work well in situations where the predictor fields are

Table 5.4: Information sought in data mining

Type of information	Explanation	Example
Association	Also referred to as correlation and relationship, association means that the occurrence of one set of items is linked to the presence of another set of items.	Find out what products sell together.
Cluster	Grouping together of items with similar characteristics.	Market segmentation.
Classification	Also referred to as rules, classification is defined as the development of a profile of each group which can be used to decide the belonging of an entity to a certain group.	Buyers of expensive sports cars are typically young, urban professional with high income.
Sequence	Also referred to sequential pattern, sequence involves events that are linked over an extended period.	Ten per cent of customers who order sheets order a comforter next.
Similar time sequence	Similar time sequence represents the discovery of sequences similar to a given time or the discovery of all pairs of similar sequences.	Finding stocks with similar price movement.
Exception	Discovering exception means finding the 'unusual'.	Detecting unusual credit card transactions.
Variance	Variance is defined as disagreement.	
Forecasting	Also referred to as pattern or trends, forecasting estimates future values based on data patterns. All the above categories of information can be used in forecasting.	Estimating future sales based on historical records.

partially irrelevant. CHAID (chi-squared automatic interaction detection) and CART (classification and regression tree) are two modelling techniques in this area. These decisions generate rules for the classification of a dataset.

- *Rule induction:* The extraction of useful 'if-then' rules from data based on statistical significance.
- *Cluster analysis:* Perhaps the most common form of data mining and is used to identify associations among data points.
- *Linkage analysis:* Linkage analysis is used to link two or more events (data points) together. Most frequently used for 'market basket' types of applications, linkage analysis can help point out associations when separate product purchases are related.
- *Time series analysis:* Time series analysis, or sequencing, is used to relate events in time. Financial analysts frequently attempt to predict interest rate fluctuations or stock performance based on a series of preceding events.
- *Categorisation analysis:* Categorisation analysis contains elements of all the aforementioned methodologies and is perhaps the most broadly applicable to different types of business problems. This method attempts to explain the influence that numerous different factors have on one specific outcome. All the data can be considered 'input' in studying a specific 'output'.

Data mining capabilities are now being evolved to integrate directly with industry-standard data warehouses and OLAP platforms by companies such as Cognos, and are also a core component of enterprise-wide software (SEM) packages and SEM business intelligence (BI).

5.7 SEM and data visualisation

Data visualisation (DV) can be defined as the process of using computer-based information systems to put business performance into a dynamic and visible form that is readily understood by users. It is concerned with the use of graphics to show the reams of data for analysis and decision-making. In its simplest form, data visualisation is in the form of bar, line, or pie charts. Spreadsheets and OLAP tools are examples of products that moderate data visualisation in business.

As the need to understand and analyse information increases, the need to explore data advances beyond simple graphics. SEM DV has the following characteristics that enable analysts to explore complex, multi-dimensional data in one screen. The functional tools associated with DV will typically include:

- filter tools for separating critical data from the mass of available data;
- view tools used to visualise filtered data;
- item tools to provide access to filtered data related to a specific product, item or business unit;
- time tools which enable the user to select relevant time periods for analysis of filtered data; and
- projection tools which enable users to view possible future outcomes based on known data.

Within the SEM approach, the presentation of strategic information is a core requirement. There is little point in providing data if it is displayed in a form that is difficult to understand. ERP vendors have already created screen designs for SEM systems that effectively use ergonomics to marry form and function. Examples include PeopleSoft's Executive Dashboard or SAP's Management Cockpit which are different terms that describe the same concept. Information is presented in ways that is most relevant to the actions that need to be reported and the decisions that need to be made.

The first level of SEM information presentation will lie in data warehouse functionality. The SAP data warehouse (SAP BW) contains a matrix style reporting function where figures are arranged in columns and rows. The second option offered by the SEM BW is to arrange the data in such a form that the user can read it as a newspaper. This concept is especially useful if textual, graphical, and tabular information is to be combined.

The maturing of multimedia software is providing authoring, and editing programs which are making it possible for SEM software vendors to create more effective visualisations. In the near future there is likely to be an increased emphasis on data visualisation functionality.

5.8 SEM analytic applications

Arthur Andersen LLP Business Consulting (1998) suggest that in order to be classified as a business intelligence (BI) analytical application, the solution must meet the following criteria:

- It structures and automates a process that helps improve business performance by embedding rules, procedures, and techniques with an accompanying methodology to solve specific business problems.

- It supports an analytic activity that examines information about the business and helps to plan for future improvements.
- It is a primary section rather than a secondary feature of an enterprise application.

Each of the SEM BI analytic applications, be they from SAP, PeopleSoft®, Oracle, Baan or any other of the major vendors, that will sit on top of existing ERP offerings will normally provide help to managers in two ways, they will:

1. structure and automate a group of tasks pertaining to the review and optimisation of business operations (process support); and
2. support the extraction, transformation, and integration of data from multiple sources, supporting time-based analysis (time-oriented, integrated data).

SEM BI analytical applications placed on top of ERP systems perform functions that change, are ad hoc, involve creativity or are linked to unexpected or unique events. The SEM BI analytical applications (such as those for planning, budgeting and forecasting) compliment the ERP systems that are already in place, thereby extending core business processes. By monitoring and analysing the latest information, businesses can detect new trends and thus respond more rapidly to changing business conditions. In this new business environment, the strategic use of information, more than the capture of information, will be the key to competitive advantage.

Many companies use spreadsheets or custom programs to gather and organise transactional data from multiple sources, but such approaches are increasingly unworkable. Spreadsheets are limited in their ability to handle complexity, and they typically do not possess the kind of core business intelligence that comes from deep industry knowledge. Custom programs require significant development and maintenance resources, and they are difficult to change when business requirements evolve.

It is fair to say that packaged solutions, like the current SEM BI offerings, present benefits that spreadsheets and custom solutions cannot match, and with the ever increasing velocity of business as well as the growing globalisation of competition, the need for accessible, comprehensive, and timely business information will continue unabated.

5.9 Concluding remarks

Few organisations have a homogenous set of source systems. Although some information will always be input manually, the aim should be to automate the collection of routine information, some of it from Internet sources. The challenge is to extract this data from diverse sources, transform it, correct it and load it into the data warehouse with as little human intervention as possible. Each additional interface will need maintenance and consequently the analytical applications should be integrated with the data warehouse, either by selecting the same supplier or by using industry-standard links.

Most organisations are more than just a single business. There may be many divisions, subsidiaries, locations, products and customers each of which may require a different level of detail for strategic decision-making. The detailed information required at the lowest levels should be compatible with the summarised requirements of higher up the organisation. The need to create a flexible environment for detailed decision-making has to be balanced against the need for consistency throughout the group and the need to take decisions that will affect several parts of the organisation at once. An effective data warehouse must be structured to allow efficient storage of information and simple and quick access. The diverse range of information needed to support an enterprise requires the gathering of data from outside of the traditional arena of the finance and logistics systems.

A data warehouse of itself is not going to significantly improve decision support within the organisation. Instead the real value of the data warehouse can only be realised when it acts as a reliable and robust data source for the range of analytical applications from OLAP to data visualisation and business intelligence.

The technologies which enable SEM continue to evolve and it is likely that the next three years will see a growing number of ERP vendors and niche software firms offering SEM capability. In the long term, competitive advantage from SEM will arise not from the adoption of widely available software or techniques, but from an organisation's ability to adopt these technologies and techniques to the unique operating and decision-making culture of the organisation.

Strategic enterprise management

6

An overview of the types of technologies on offer from vendors

6.1 Introduction

In the past few years, the focus of business applications has shifted from transaction processing (getting data in) to the decision support (getting information out). The goal of this has been to enable managers to manipulate and emphasise the data most relevant to them. At the same time reporting has moved from traditional hard-copy printed reports to having information on screen with the ability to drill down to the underlying data or to share it with other managers using web-type technologies.

Many organisations acquired ERP solutions in the hope of improving both their decision support and their reporting processes. Although there has been a great deal of debate and controversy pertaining to the management reporting capabilities of ERP systems, a large number of organisations are still investing heavily in ERP systems in the hope of improving their reporting capabilities. Originally it was thought that a single, highly-integrated ERP system would meet the information needs of all the managers in the organisation. However, it was soon realised that this would be too complex to implement and so now many experts favour a series of integrated subsystems with, in some cases, different vendors offering different functionality. This best of breed strategy is gaining momentum and many ERP vendors themselves are forming strategic partnerships with the providers of analytical applications to deliver the best combinations to the end client.

All the indications are that ERP systems by themselves do not lead to a significant improvement in analysis and reporting capabilities. Most companies have supplemented their ERP systems with analytic applications which allow executives to leverage the value of the detailed transaction data in the ERP systems. Analytic applications maximise and extend the investment that has already been made in an ERP system. As such they complement the ERP transactional data, by extending the reach of management right back to the core business processes. By monitoring and analysing the latest information, businesses can detect new trends and respond more rapidly to changing business conditions. Thus it facilitates the strategic use of information to configure and monitor the business model in search of competitive advantage.

Organisations need to understand the SEM market-place (see Figure 6.1) and think strategically in order to be successful in deploying SEM technologies. The SEM technologies that are currently available have four essential characteristics:

1.   information capture (the ability to collect data);
2.   information storage (the ability to retain data);
3.   information manipulation (the ability to process data); and
4.   information distribution (the ability to transmit data electronically).

In this chapter we explore the different offerings available under these four categories of SEM functionality. The review of the SEM products on offer is not intended to be a comprehensive benchmark study but rather is designed to give the reader an insight into the typical offerings in each sector of the SEM technology market-place.

6.2 Information capture – ERP and other data capture solutions

SEM analytical applications will need to access a wide variety of data sources. These will include information from traditional ERP systems as well as from emerging customer relationship management (CRM) and e-commerce sources, see Figure 6.2. In recent years there has been a considerable consolidation in many of these markets with the large ERP vendors such as SAP, Oracle and PeopleSoft® extending their functionality into CRM and e-commerce. As well as developing their own solutions in each area, ERP vendors are also providing functionality through integration with best of breed products in each area.

6.2.1 Internal rusting legacy data sources

Many firms still have a large number of legacy systems that support day-to-day operations. These will typically be written in older languages such as Cobol, or in third generation environments such as RPG, PL1, etc. In addition firms may have applications developed in early fourth generation

Figure 6.1: The SEM software market-place

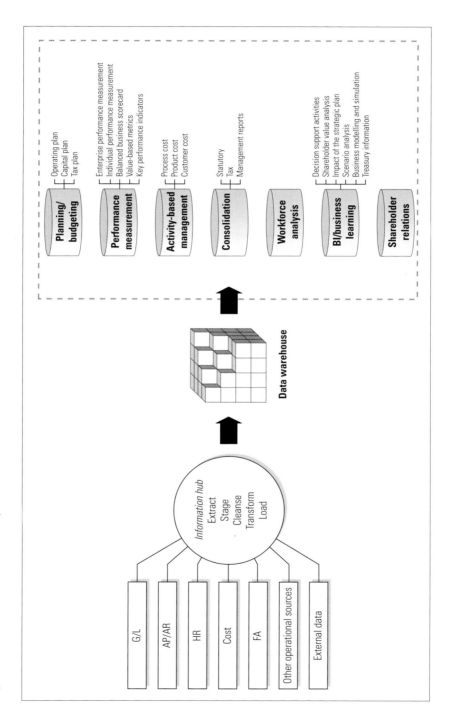

SQL database environments using tools such as Focus, Informix, etc. Over time these applications may be replaced by ERP solutions but in the interim the firm will have to develop extraction and integration processes to ensure that the valuable data contained in these systems is not lost. The single biggest challenge which firms face in extracting data from these applications is often the poor quality of the systems documentation.

Figure 6.2: The range of data sources

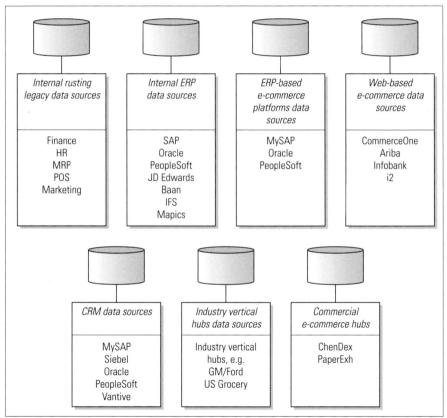

6.2.2 *Internal ERP data sources*

Over the past two years, these markets have matured to a point where most major vendors have been able to deliver standard functionality across all the major vertical industry markets and integrated coverage of all major functional areas. Among the most important attributes of ERP data capture systems are their ability to:

- automate and integrate with the majority of an organisation's business processes;
- share common data and practices across the entire enterprise;
- produce and access information in a real-time environment;
- have multi-country, multilingual, and multi-currency capabilities that conforms to diverse legal and fiscal standards;
- support the major database formats, either by internal architecture, or by using Open DataBase Connectivity (ODBC);
- interface easily with third party products;
- support 'componentised' architecture;
- support a variety of user interfaces;
- support external business flows, from suppliers and to customers in the 'global supply chain'; and
- support internet and intranet-based activities including business to business (B2B), business to consumer (B2C) and business to employee (B2E).

Four main firms currently dominate the market-place for ERP solutions. Their standings are summarised in Table 6.1.

Table 6.1: The main firms in the ERP market-place.

SAP	Number one vendor of standard business application software
	Industry-based solution sets
	Dominates industries such as CPG, manufacturing, and chemicals
	Strong commitment to R&D (16 per cent of annual revenue)
	Expansion with functional, industry and geographic initiatives
PeopleSoft®	Strong HRM/payroll and finance functionality as well as CRM
	Highest client satisfaction rating among ERP vendors
	Excellent presence/reputation in services and insurance industries
	New customers represent majority of new licenses fees
Oracle	Strong and mature database management system and tools
	Best of breed strategy in past
	Positioning towards Internet and CRM space
JD Edwards	Strong finance and distribution systems
	Consumer packaged goods (CPG) industry strength
	Strong middle market presence new client/server product
	Well positioned in 'new battleground'

© PricewaterhouseCoopers.

6.2.3 ERP-based e-commerce platforms

The top ERP vendors have devoted large amounts of resources to providing e-commerce and CRM functionality as part of their product offerings. In the e-commerce space, Oracle has made significant inroads and claims to have captured a substantial portion of the *Fortune* 100 firms as clients. The smaller second tier ERP vendors such as IFS, Mapics, Baan and others are at the moment offering limited e-commerce capability based mainly around e-procurement/e-fulfilment. At the core of the ERP based e-commerce platforms is a move to web-based portals for interfacing with suppliers, employees and customers.

6.2.4 Web-based e-commerce data sources

These are specialist software applications developed specifically to provide e-commerce capability in what are typically B2B environments. The main software players in this market are listed in Table 6.2. A number of these vendors have strategic partnerships with established ERP vendors and over time it is expected that this market space will see significant rationalisation and consolidation as the major ERP vendors, such as SAP and Oracle, build up their development efforts.

Table 6.2: Sample list of e-commerce solution providers

Ariba Technologies	www.ariba.com
Clarus Corp	www.claruscorp.com
Commerce One	www.commerceone.com
Elcom International	www.elcom.com
Infobank	www.infobank.co.uk
Intelisys	www.intelisys.com
Tradezone	www.Tradezone.com
Trilogy.com	www.trilogy.com
i2	www.i2.com

6.2.5 CRM data sources

Sales force automation, CRM systems and contact management are all different names that refer to the application of computers and databases to improving or supporting the process of selling and managing customer relationships. In recent years a number of software vendors have begun offering 'solutions' in this market space. Leaders include Siebel Systems (www.siebel.com), Oracle (www.oracle.com) and SAP. PeopleSoft® (www.peoplesoft.com/crm) have recently been endorsed by a number of leading authorities as the leader in the field through its acquisition of Vantive and its successful web integration strategy.

6.2.6 Industry vertical hubs as data sources

In a number of industries firms have come together to establish industry specific e-commerce hubs for trading purposes. These on-line markets or exchanges are typically owned by a number of firms in the industry, and suppliers or buyers use the on-line market to execute business transactions. While a firm may not be in a position to be a founder member of a hub, such as the automotive sector, it may have little choice but to participate in the on-line market if it wishes to supply to firms in that industry. In the coming years these industry markets are likely to become an established source of transaction data for most firms. Table 6.3 gives examples of these hubs and also independent commercial hubs. In most cases the hubs in question use one of the established ERP e-commerce platforms, such as Oracle or MySap.com, or else one of the specialist web-based platforms, such as Ariba.

Table 6.3: Examples of industry vertical hubs and commercial hubs

Industry	E-market
Aerospace and defence	Exostar
Auto manufacturing	GM/Covisint
Consumer products	Transora
Energy/petrochemicals	Petrocosm
Energy/petrochemicals	Trade Ranger
High tech	e2open
High tech	Ehitex
Pharmaceuticals	PharmaExchange
Retail	GlobalNetXchange
Retail	WWRE
Telecommunications	Telco Exchange
Utilities	Pantellos

6.2.7 *Commercial e-commerce hubs as data sources*

These are hubs which are generally independent of any particular industry player. The hub operates using either an exchange or auction model and charges fees per transaction or on a percentage basis. As with the industry vertical hubs the commercial hub is normally based on an established ERP e-commerce or one of the specialist web-based platforms.

6.3 Information storage – data warehousing

The market for data warehousing software is expected to grow dramatically in the next three years. The Data Warehousing Institute predicts an average increase of 43 per cent each year to 2003.

6.3.1 *Specialist data warehousing vendors*

As with the ERP market, a small number of vendors account for a significant portion of the total market. In addition, the established vendors are under pressure from the ERP providers who are including so called warehousing solutions as part of their product offerings. Table 6.4 summarises some of the vendors who provide software in the data warehousing area.

6.3.2 *Data warehousing offerings from ERP vendors*

While Oracle has a long track record in providing database solutions, both PeopleSoft® and SAP were rather late entrants to the data warehousing market. As a database firm of over twenty years standing Oracle has a large installed base of users. Its data warehousing technology is built on a solid relational database management system track record and the firm's offerings are very popular with software developers. In addition the large installed base makes integration with other platforms easier and there is a significant (if expensive) supply of expertise available. Oracle has had a reputation for explicitly supporting a best of breed approach to SEM, and its SEM architecture illustrates this by showing a large number of non-Oracle components.

Table 6.4: Data warehousing software vendors

Solution Area	Product	Vendor
Report and query	BrioQuery	Brio Technology
	Impromptu	Cognos
	Business Objects	Business Objects
	Crystal Reports	Seagate Software
OLAP/MD analysis	DSS Agent/Server	Microstrategy
	DecisionSuite	Information Advantage
	EssBase	Hyperion Solutions
	Express Server	Oracle
	PowerPlay	Cognos
	Brio Enterprise	Brio Technology
	Business Objects	Business Objects
Data mining	Discovery Server	Pilot Software
	Intelligent Miner	IBM
	Darwin	Oracle
	SAS System	SAS Institute
Data modelling	ER/Win	Computer Associates
Data ETL	Data Propagator	IBM
	InfoPump	Platinum Technology
	Integrity Data Re-Eng	Vality Technology
	Warehouse Manager	Prism Solutions
	PowerMart	Informatica
Databases for data warehousing	DB2	IBM
	Oracle Server	Oracle
	MS SQL Server	Microsoft
	Redbrick Warehouse	Red Brick Corp.
	Teradata DBS	NCR
Information catalogue	DataGuide	IBM
	HP Intelligent Warehouse: Guide	Hewlett-Packard
	Directory Manager	Prism Solutions

The technical basis for SAP SEM is the SAP Business Information Warehouse (SAP BW). The SAP BW stores the metadata and application data for all SAP SEM components and provides the mechanisms for read and write access, and data collection. An important characteristic of SAP SEM is the integration of the metadata and application data of all SAP SEM components in a unified data basis. All components read their working data from there and also write the resulting data there. Under the SAP approach the structured data, for example from the ERP system, continues to form an important part of the information supply for the strategic management process. SAP emphasises the point that the extraction of data from its R/3 and R/4 ERP software is particularly easy with SAP BW. In the case of R/3 is has well-developed extractors for all R/3 components. While there is a clear single vendor tone to the SAP BW offering, the firm does point out that it is much simpler to set up comprehensive data transfer between an installed R/3 system and SAP SEM than between a third-party system and SAP SEM. To collect data from third-party systems, it recommends the use of third-party tools or the development and application of a firm's own programs to handle the SAP BW interface.

The PeopleSoft Enterprise Warehouse™ is the single point of reference for the entire Enterprise Performance Management solution. It functions as the central data repository, collecting data from an organisations ERP and non-ERP systems, storing analytic application-enhanced data, and feeding the balanced scorecard and Workbench reporting templates. PeopleSoft® chose Informatica's PowerMart as their tool to perform the extracting, transformation and loading of data into their Enterprise Warehouse (EW). As such PeopleSoft® has an Extract Transform and Load tool that has the capability to extract data from the data store of all major source systems (i.e. Oracle, DB2, Sybase, Flat File, etc.) including DB2/390. As part of its data warehousing offering PeopleSoft® has also included interfaces to Crystal Reports, Hyperion Essbase™, Cognos Powerplay™ and others. In keeping with the best of breed approach it appears more willing than SAP to facilitate a pluralistic approach to data warehousing. In its acquisition of CRM software Vantive, PeopleSoft also increased its data warehousing expertise and this is reflected in very positive reviews from data warehousing experts such as Bill Inmon the so called father of data warehousing.

6.3.3 *Hyperion EssBase™ – a favourite with finance professionals*

Established in 1981, Hyperion Software is the world's leading provider of financially-related analytic applications. The company's focus is on designing financial software applications that allow finance professionals to access and distribute information, and measure and analyse the performance of the business. The company has a long track record in multi-source consolidation and management reporting, and it has developed core expertise in allowing large, multinational companies to maintain a single global view of financial information across multiple sites. Hyperion Essbase™ is the leading OLAP technology which underpins the Hyperion analytical applications. As a data warehousing tool it has been optimised for enterprise management reporting, analysis and planning applications. In particular, Hyperion Essbase™ supports multi-user read/write access, large-scale data capacity, robust analytical calculations, and sophisticated OLAP queries. It is particularly popular with finance professionals who have adopted it for use in many planning and budgeting applications.

The list of firms that have adopted Essbase as a data warehouse to support their management planning and control activities to date is very impressive and it is likely that Hyperion will continue to attract a loyal following in the SEM market space. Firms that have used Essbase to date include FedEx, John Deere, and Sprint. Essbase is particularly popular in a best of breed setting as outlined in Figure 6.3. Under this approach a finance function will often choose Essbase over established vendors such as Oracle because of its unique finance analysis and reporting functionality.

Any decision on a data warehouse to support the SEM architecture needs to be supported by an extensive review of the market offerings. In particular it should include an assessment of the different vendors offerings under the headings of:

- data acquisition;
- primary storage;
- analytical applications;
- data delivery; and
- metadata management.

Figure 6.3: Hyperion Essbase™ in a best of breed setting.

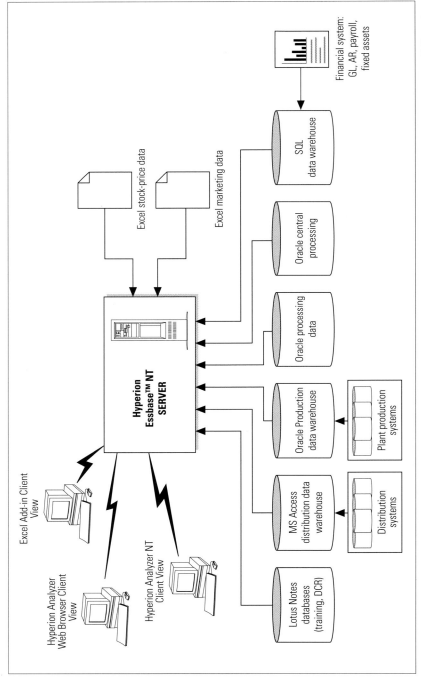

© Hyperion.

6.4 Information manipulation – analytical applications

In this section the functionality of some of the analytical applications available in the SEM market is explored. Once again it must be stressed that the specific examples used are designed to illustrate generic capability rather than as an endorsement of a particular vendor.

6.4.1 Activity-based management

The specialist ABC/M software market has developed steadily over the past decade. Software packages fall into three groups:

1. Software developed by the major consulting firms such as Deloitte, KPMG, and PricewaterhouseCoopers (PwC), which is promoted by them to support their consulting efforts.
2. Software developed by independent software houses, such as Armstrong Laing whose product is Hyper ABC, Lawson Software whose product is Lawson Insight, Sapling Corp. whose product is NetProphet, and ABC Technologies whose product is Oros ABC plus.
3. Constituent modules of enterprise resource software packages, such as SAP or Baan Triton.

Oros® from ABCTECH brings together a significant amount of ABC/M functionality in a single product. The Oros® suite includes:

- Oros® Analytics for Planning – scenario analysis.
- Oros® Analytics for Profit – profitability analysis by product, service, customer, region, channel, etc.
- Oros® Analytics for Cost Management – determine the costs of products, services, activities or business processes.
- Oros® Scorecard – balanced scorecard.

Table 6.5: Sample of ABC solution vendors

Vendor	Product
ABC Technologies	Oros®
Armstrong Laing	MetifyABC
Decimal Lead Technology	ABM Tools
Technologies, Inc	CMS
ICMS	Value Stream Manager
Interactive Process Management	Activity Analyzer
Mevatec	FastTrack ABM
Sapling	Net Prophet
Oracle	Activa
Prodacapo	

The ABC/M capability is delivered mainly through the analytics for profit and the analytics for cost management. At the heart of the product is a modelling tool which allows organisations to create detailed models of their value chain or any individual process. The product comes with a large number of pre-set input templates and wizards, which help in documenting the firms processes and activities. The Oros® suite provides rich functionality including:

- process-driven import wizards that facilitate rapid exchange and merging of data formats;
- bi-directional integration with ERP systems and ODBC-compliant databases;
- large account and account hierarchy capacity;
- user-defined periods;
- flow cost information using a variety of drivers including basic, weighted, calculated and multidimensional drivers;
- 'point and click' cost assignment creation;
- multi-model consolidation capabilities;
- scenario planning and analysis with bi-directional connection with Microsoft Excel;
- direct integration with SAP SEM Business Planning and Simulation and SAP R/3 Costing Information through Oros®;
- step-by-step, multidimensional profitability analysis capabilities;
- on-screen variance analysis to quickly identify key areas of interest;

- powerful 'what-if' scenario analysis;
- account trending and forecasting;
- data filtering/selection criteria for reporting;
- standard and multi-model reporting;
- report publishing in .html format; and
- pinpoint analysis of data through the automated creation of OLAP databases including connections with: Cognos PowerPlay™, SAS CFO Vision™ and Hyperion Essbase™.

6.4.2 Consolidation

When important financial reporting information resides in multiple general ledgers, systems, and spreadsheets, consolidating information from these different sources can be inefficient and time consuming. In situations where the consolidation process is not automated, information must be manually keyed in from printed reports, a tedious and error-prone approach. In the absence of a streamlined consolidation process, finance professionals end up spending large amounts of time scrubbing large data sets in an attempt to deliver accurate monthly and quarterly reports.

An analysis of the time spent on key consolidation tasks shows that much consolidation function time is still spent on low value-added activities, such as re-keying data, chasing late and incorrect business unit returns and reconciling data.

Table 6.6: Types of consolidation tool

Category	Tools
Specialised systems	Commander FDC, Hyperion Micro-Control, Hyperion Enterprise
ERP package/GL	Coda, GEAC, JDA, Lawson, Oracle, PeopleSoft®, Platinum, SAP®, QSP
OLAP	Essbase, TMI, Timeline

A recent PwC survey of global consolidation practices shows that the introduction of enterprise-wide global charts of account has not resulted in a wide use of ERP/general ledger systems for consolidation. PwC found that only 19 per cent of those who are implementing global charts of account are using an ERP system, such as SAP, or general ledger package to consolidate. In many cases firms have reported that many of the

Table 6.7: Review of sample consolidation systems

Hyperion Hyperion Enterprise was released in 1991 and is now in its fifth major release. It is an advanced business information consolidation and reporting application designed to provide a unified view of accounting information across diverse general ledgers for management reporting, tax and statutory reporting requirements. Hyperion Enterprise is the leading financial consolidation, reporting and analysis solution. It is used by more than 3500 organisations. Hyperion Enterprise is unique in its ability to handle the wide range of financial consolidation and reporting requirements under US GAAP, International Accounting Standards (IAS), and other local and regional accounting requirements. The product is designed to allow companies to handle the detailed line of business information required for management reporting purposes while also meeting complex legal/statutory and tax reporting requirements.

Functionality includes: ◆ FAS52 currency conversion; ◆ intercompany eliminations; ◆ FAS94 minority interest consolidations; ◆ European Monetary Union (EMU) dual currency reporting; ◆ supports six languages; ◆ integration with ERP and other data sources.

SAP Business Consolidation (SEM-BCS) from SAP can be used for both the statutory (external) consolidation and the management (internal) consolidation. SEM-BCS is based on the uniform data basis of the SEM system and benefits, therefore, from the flexibility of the entire system when defining organisational units and hierarchical structures.

Functionality includes: ◆ support for all required functions for the legal consolidation according to existing statutory accounting requirements US-GAAP, IAS, local GAAPs, etc.; ◆ intercompany/unit eliminations; ◆ consolidation within groups including reporting of multiple company hierarchies; ◆ integration with ERP and other data sources; ◆ foreign currency translation.

CLIME CLIME is a PwC supported product which focuses almost exclusively on providing consolidation functionality to large multinational organisations. It comes with a variety of data entry and validation options to suit every purpose, including the automatic import from client financial and operational systems, data input through user-defined data entry screens and automatic feeds from spreadsheets. CLIME uses a multidimensional database that goes beyond conventional OLAP to create, store and manage all of the data required for group reporting. In addition to storing the traditional account balances for each company, period, currency and version combination, CLIME has multidimensionality to store information by customer, product stream, cost centre and so on.

In addition it has the following functionality: ◆ calculation of periodic/cumulative data; ◆ foreign currency translation; ◆ intercompany matching and automatic elimination of intercompany differences; ◆ easy creation and reporting of multiple company hierarchies; ◆ processes to support head office and multiple divisional reporting; ◆ it also supports third party products such as Cognos PowerPlay™.

ERP/general ledger packages do not yet have sufficient levels of functionality. The same survey reported that 43 per cent of firms were using specialised systems, 12 per cent were using spreadsheets and a further 21 per cent were using in-house customised solutions.

6.4.3 Planning and budgeting

Companies engage in planning and budgeting to establish corporate-wide commitment to a plan and provide a standard to evaluate progress against that plan. Unfortunately, for most organisations, the budgeting process tends to be enormously expensive and time-consuming, often commanding several months and numerous iterations. Companies are finding that their conventional budgeting approaches have failed to keep pace with the demands of the market-place.

In addition, given the pace of change in the market-place, unforeseen events can quickly outdate budgets, and firms must increasingly rely on shorter-term forecasting to keep them on course for target earnings. Without a flexible forecasting/planning system, firms risk missing important shifts in the competitive dynamic which can damage long-term shareholder value.

A large number of firms offer planning and budgeting applications and some of these are listed in Table 6.8.

Table 6.8: Planning and budgeting software

Vendor	*Product name*
ABCTech	Oros® Analytics for Planning
Hyperion	Pillar
Frango	Budget Advisor
Comshare	Comshare MPC™
Cognos™	Cognos Finance
Powersim	Powersim Integrated Analytics™
Great Plains	FRx Forecaster
Prodacapo	Prodacapo Business Planning Manager

Hyperion Pillar is the market-leading budgeting application used by more than 2300 companies worldwide. Hyperion Pillar supports a range of planning and budgeting tasks ranging from activity-based budgeting and project-based planning, to capital planning, sales forecasting and compensation planning. Product functionality includes:

- *Distributed architecture* – Pillar supports both remote and disconnected users, and allows large numbers of users to work on their budgets independently but simultaneously.
- *Detailed plan creation* – Hyperion Pillar allows line managers to plan using business drivers such as units, rates and amounts.
- *Modelling and analysis* – managers can create relationships among data elements in a plan without building macros or formulas into spreadsheets.
- *Advanced process management* – once line managers complete and submit their individual budgets, financial and consolidation level managers can automatically view the results in their overall plans.
- *Integration with ERP and other data sources* – via application programming interfaces (APIs) companies can extend the budgeting functionality of Hyperion Pillar through integration with ERP, and other third-party applications.

Many organisations use Hyperion Pillar in conjunction with Hyperion Essbase™ for extended reporting, analysis modelling and planning.

6.5 Information presentation and distribution

A number of areas can be included under this general heading of information presentation and distribution. Very few of the software vendors offer a single piece of presentation software with most incorporating the data presentation element in a number of their product modules. For example, Cognos™ provides information presentation through Cognos Visualizer™, Impromptu™ and Upfront™. In addition, firms such as Hyperion are using portal technology to exploit the web to give users customised access to information.

Table 6.9 summarises some of the products which are available in this market space. In the future there is likely to be an increased emphasis on the presentation and distribution aspects with a general move to more web-enabled approaches to publishing and distributing information to users.

Table 6.9: Products that support information presentation

Vendor	Product
Cognos™	Powerplay™, Visualizer™, Impromptu™, Upfront™
Comshare	Comshare FDC™
Frango	Frango (Web Reports, Report Books and EIS)
MIS AG	MIS Alea
SunSystems	SunSystems 5
Hyperion	Hyperion Enterprise, Hyperion Performance Management
Great Plains	Enterprise reporting, e-enterprise reporter
Prodacapo	Balanced Scorecard Manager
ABC Tech	Oros® Scorecard
SAP	Corporate Performance Monitor
PeopleSoft®	Balanced Scorecard

SAP SEM has adopted one of the more innovative approaches to information presentation with its corporate performance monitoring module. As part of this SAP offers a decision room technology called the Management Cockpit™. The Management Cockpit™ software is included in the SEM package. The software's features include:

- definition of numerous Cockpit scenarios;
- management of access authorisations for Cockpit configurations;
- structuring of performance indicators on four walls for four perspectives;
- each wall covering one topic and having an assigned colour;
- assignment of up to six logical views per wall;
- assignment of up to six frames per logical view;
- frames visualising performance indicators using:
  - tachometer graphics,
  - horizontal bar charts,
  - four-quadrant matrices,
  - portfolio graphics,
  - standard business graphics;
- traffic light reporting.

6.6 Some concluding remarks

It is impossible in a chapter such as this to identify all the products on offer. Each month new products appear and existing firms, such as Hyperion, are continually adding new functionality. In addition firms are exploiting strategic partnerships to provide a best of breed approach which allows firms to 'clip together' a range of software applications which best meet their needs. A number of independent research firms, such as Gartner, AMR, Forrester, etc., provide research reports on many of the software applications discussed in this chapter. It is worthwhile maintaining a watching brief on these research reports. The most useful insights, however, will often come from discussions with finance professionals in other organisations who are using the product in question. It is important therefore that accountants develop and contribute to a wide professional network of contacts that can share these valuable insights. In this regard attending short presentations and conferences can provide the tips and tricks, which are very often a critical success factor in making the right software choices.

The learning is in the doing 7

SEM as a process and a management competency

7.1 Introduction

In the past bad information has undoubtedly led to bad decisions. In particular executives have had to rely on 'gut feel' and intuition when they would have preferred to have access to more objective information. In particular executives have in the past complained about 'black-holes' in the information they are provided with for decision-making purposes. As a result management need to take 'blind' decisions for significant parts of the working cycle, due to lack of information. Over time decisions can become arbitrary.

In many firms executives currently pose large numbers of questions that cannot be effectively answered due to information limitations in the current environment. Unless there is a dramatic improvement in the decision support offered by the finance function, the gap between the information and analysis available versus that which is required will continue to grow.

CFO challenges identified by PwC in its look at the finance function in the 21st century include:

- too much reporting and not enough analysis;
- manually intense process;
- data is not available;
- data is not standardised;
- existing systems are not user-friendly;
- lack of data integration and integrity;
- unstable technical environment;
- existing tools cannot handle dynamic environment; and
- Excel and calculators are the standard.

7.2　New finance skills and systems

Finance staff often see themselves as possessing certain core skills from which they derive business value. These include high intellect, technical excellence, and prompt delivery. In addition, they often claim to be under-valued by the business. On the other hand business managers complain that finance staff are:

● unresponsive;
● do not understand the business;
● speak jargon when asked for clear insights;
● obsessed with bureaucratic processes; and
● produce the same data month in/out.

A recent benchmarking survey by KPMG found that:

● 87 per cent of CEOs believe finance must become a business partner or leader in the next three to five years;
● only 56 per cent think finance is already a business partner, and are they really?
● only 42 per cent of the participants have defined the vision or mission of the role of finance;
● only 32 per cent of participants are re-engineering finance processes; and
● only 30 per cent of finance organisations use performance metrics to measure performance of finance processes.

Many of the difficulties associated with the finance function arise from the focus on traditional transaction processing which occupies most accountants on a day-to-day basis (see Figure 7.1). As a result of this internal process focus they often lose sight of the need for them to become business partners in the creation of shareholder value.

To be really effective at dealing with strategic business issues, two things are required: a thorough understanding of the business, and financial awareness. There is a clear need for the finance function to move away from its old structures and to instead organise along the value chain. This involves moving away from the traditional focus on internal controls/transaction process and towards a new finance culture.

Figure 7.1: The internal business focus of finance professionals

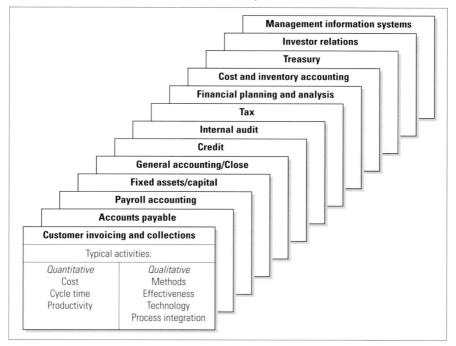

7.2.1 Strategic orientation

If finance staff are to develop a true SEM capability, they need to take a more constructive role as part of the management team in the operation of the business and become more closely involved in decision-making. In practice this means:

- Proactively suggest options in business decision-making rather than merely evaluating strategic investment decisions. Understanding the behaviour of costs with respect to changing volumes and market conditions including which activities, products and customers are adding value and which are not.
- Evaluating the firms and SBU performance and review its strategies on a continuous basis, helping communicate strategic objectives to employees in a manner which allows them to operationalise strategy. Using their analytical skills to unlock the value in customer and cost information in evaluating proposals.
- Monitor the progress towards strategic goals through performance tracking measures.

- Fine tune and re-configure the business model in the face of competition and help build a culture of value creation in the organisation.
- Evaluate new initiatives to achieve profitable growth.
- Move to a system of allocation of resources on the basis of value creation.

7.2.2 *Effective performance measurement and reporting*

Openly available information can be a powerful driver of improved corporate and business unit performance. In the past ERP systems have failed to meet managers' information needs. As a result there was often a proliferation of spreadsheets or manually driven personal systems to gather information and report. As a result in a significant number of organisations, essential management information is created and locked away in spreadsheets. Spreadsheets are useful general purpose tools but in many cases they should be replaced by SEM solutions, which are easier to maintain and which provide the features needed as standard. The information in spreadsheets may also be inconsistent, inaccessible to those who need the information, and are manually updated so prone to error. Effective SEM performance measurement and reporting is characterised by:

- Providing executives and management with the cost information needed to assess profitability across the dimensions of product, customers and channels.
- Performance parameters that reflect business and strategy and the core processes that underlie it.
- Continuous communication of financial information to management where information and advice flows in a continuous feedback loop.
- Presentation of information is driven by user requirements using media which supports flexing and modelling when appropriate.
- There is decentralised access to performance information and results.
- Insightful commentary is provided with or prior to results and not after them.
- Linking performance measures to the fundamental drivers of value and in turn linking compensation to shareholder value.

Balance is required to ensure that the full picture is obtained while avoiding measures. Finance staff need to ensure that the measures are defined using several perspectives: financial and non-financial, predictive and historical, external and internal.

7.2.3 *Systems and data management*

A key concept underpinning SEM is the existence of a single underlying data source that can be used for each of the analytical applications. The reality of most organisations is a multitude of different operational systems. Although some information will always be input manually, the aim should be to automate the collection of routine information. The challenge is to extract this data from diverse sources, transform it, correct it and load it into the data warehouse with as little manual intervention as possible. The characteristics of effective SEM systems and data management include:

- Fully automated data delivery to the analytical applications with systematic front-end-data validation based on a single data-flow for closing and reporting.
- Data suppliers should be responsible for data accuracy with procedures fully documented and understood. Ideally detailed transaction data for costing purposes should also be accessible. Coding schemes should capture costs in a way that makes them directly attributed to activities and cost object.
- Integrate and store information within a central repository to synchronise management reporting across multiple dimensions.
- External and non-financial data that provides the balanced view of performance are often not available in the same format as internal financial information. Until the interface between these data sources can be improved it may be necessary to use sample data.
- Capture/consolidate link data from multiple sources by developing a repeatable, end-to-end, process for transforming data into information.
- There should be a detailed underlying IS/IT strategy which includes a specific plan for the integration of SEM with core systems. As such SEM will require an appropriate and efficient IT infrastructure. Only then can information be drawn from a variety of source systems and be consistent.
- The interfaces to the analytical applications need to be designed in a way which allows them to be changed quickly by users. If these changes cannot be done by easily, staff are likely to slip back in to the habit of using shadow spreadsheet-based systems.
- The detailed information required at the lowest levels should be compatible with the summarised requirements higher up the organisation.
- Extend existing legacy, ERP and data warehouse solutions and reduce paper-based reporting, deploying more quickly and cost effectively with web-enabled tools.

7.2.4 *Business awareness and commercial acumen*

In the past finance staff have paid too much attention to external reporting requirements and have exhibited low levels of operational/business awareness. In addition many have only a very elementary understanding of the value creation process and limited appreciation of the important role played by intangible assets and knowledge-based resources. To effectively deploy SEM systems, finance staff need to learn to manage information and decision support processes more effectively, so that executives can obtain reliable information and engage in more efficient scenario assessment. This involves more forward looking systems which incorporate value-based decision-making approaches. In addition, however, finance professionals must themselves change and in particular they need to have:

● Excellent analytical skills using not just financial analysis, but customer/market analysis, statistical and in some cases more sophisticated modelling techniques including simulation.

● Use of multi-disciplinary team approach to inform key decision-making (e.g. investment, marketing). Including the ability to integrate inputs from diverse experts.

● Strong commercial acumen characterised by strong product, process and market knowledge.

● Effective interpersonal skills which allow them to adopt a more consultative approach.

● A strong coaching ability which helps managers to be more focused on adding value.

● A forward looking perspective where they appreciate value rather than cost.

● An openness to the sharing of best practice and a willingness to partner with the business managers.

7.3 The SEM implementation process

There is overwhelming anecdotal and scientific evidence to suggest that firms have struggled to improve their SEM systems. While the promotional material for systems vendors abounds with case studies of successful projects the landscape is littered with projects that have failed to meet expectations.

The successful implementation of a SEM system in a large organisation requires a well-designed and executed implementation process. In particular it requires a process which is sympathetic to the unique needs of the

Figure 7.2: A new culture for the finance function

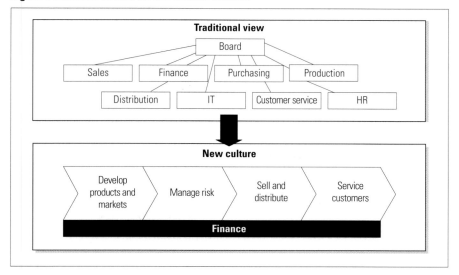

organisation, but which fully leverages the power of the best practice processes which are implicit in SEM. While no two implementations will be the same, a number of well-defined phases or steps in the process can be identified. In this section we explore the nature of the implementation process and provide an insight into the work to be carried out during each phase and the expected deliverables. Completing the activities in the proposed approach will help the company develop its SEM vision.

Before embarking on an expensive and time-consuming process, organisations need to clearly understand the effort involved in migrating to an SEM approach. In particular it is important that the senior executives in the firm are aware of the scope and size of the project and the associated risks.

Numerous surveys of the finance function have shown that the significant benefits which ERP systems are capable of achieving are not currently being achieved in practice. Making major changes to something as large and complicated as the analysis and reporting systems of an organisation is not something that can be achieved in a short timeframe. A SEM project tries to leverage the company's existing ERP systems, investment and capabilities to significantly increase the effectiveness of the firms strategic management processes. As such the SEM project puts in place the ongoing processes which will deliver the continuous insights and therefore enable executives to increase shareholder value for the company.

The SEM implementation approach should be highly interactive with continuous finance staff involvement ensuring skill transfer and development of new SEM 'champions'. It should promote the use of benchmarking and 'best practices' concepts to facilitate continuous change within the finance organisation, and challenge the organisation to look at finance as a value creation process rather than as an expense.

The purpose of the framework is to support the development of a realistic agenda for exploiting the opportunities offered by SEM technologies in a way which will create the most value for the enterprise and its shareholders.

The framework is designed to enable finance professionals to provide a rapid assessment of how effectively the organisation is applying its current SEM capability. The overall aim is to maximise the level of business value derived from the SEM system.

The framework has six phases. Within each phase are a number of tasks. A variety of inputs will be involved to achieve several deliverables for each of the phases. These inputs include senior management interviews, surveys, process walkthroughs and technology reviews.

7.3.1 Phase 1: Creating and discovering – identifying the SEM opportunities

The primary aim of this phase is to confirm the organisation's current SEM systems and processes and its overall level of SEM capability. This phase involves a high level review of processes and systems to identify key opportunity areas and material gaps between the requirements of management and the supporting SEM environment. This will determine the focus for efforts in later phases when more detailed assessments will be carried out. The intention is that this phase will be relatively brief (one to four weeks, depending on the size of the organisation). Phase 1 will involve some or all of the following tasks:

- preliminary review of SEM processes and systems, including detailed SEM process decomposition;
- assess SEM alignment with executive committee requirements;
- review the organisation's ERP/ IT infrastructure;
- review use and effectiveness of available SEM functionality;
- review SEM capability and compare to benchmarks;
- conduct workshops and focus groups to identify opportunities for improvement;

- compare results to identify performance gaps, issues and opportunities;
- consolidate issues and perform root cause analysis where required; and
- identify improvement opportunities and remedies for any gaps or issues.

An important purpose of this phase is to gauge the current position of the enterprise relative to benchmarks and best practices. The organisation's SEM approach is evaluated at the detailed process level. The intention of this phase is to highlight areas where the current performance is particularly weak at an early stage in the SEM project. This will enable efforts to be focussed on weaker areas where the potential improvements and returns are greatest. A significant effort will normally be devoted to the identification of performance and capability improvements that may be made in the technical infrastructure. However, in reviewing the performance of the organisation, four areas will normally be assessed; systems, processes, people and climate for change.

Figure 7.3: Change management in the SEM environment

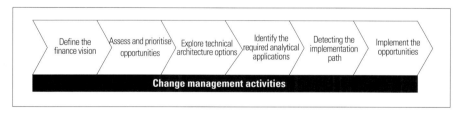

7.3.2 *Phase 2: Sharing and learning – prioritise opportunities*

The prioritising of opportunities will involve an examination of the issues and gaps highlighted by the first phase. Process, technological and people issues are considered. Improvement opportunities are identified. Recommendations and solutions are proposed, considered and grouped together into viable projects. The associated risks and implementation barriers are assessed and the solutions are validated with the client. Preliminary cost benefit analyses are carried out where appropriate and the strategic and tactical importance of projects is assessed.

Several deliverables are created in this phase. Improvement opportunities are quantified in terms of cost and estimated return and a list of general and specific recommendations and benefits is produced. A business case is developed for high priority projects. The impact of the expected improvements and strategic and tactical importance of each project is normally considered. The main work product from this final phase is the refined list of potential projects, for which initial approval can be obtained. In addition outputs might include:

- Build detailed business cases for high probability projects.
- Develop specific recommendations or identify appropriate solutions.
- Group recommendations/solutions and build appropriate projects.
- Validate solutions, assess risks and implementation barriers with firm input.
- Refine proposed project solutions.
- Prioritise projects for detailed business case development and implementation planning.

At the end of this stage an implementation plan and schedule should be developed for the SEM project and an overall integrated change plan for a portfolio of viable projects developed.

7.3.3 Phase 3: Determine the technical architecture

The technical architecture of SEM is well established even at this early stage in its development. As Figure 7.4 illustrates the core issue is one of deploying a data warehouse and its associated analytical applications.

Throughout the history of systems development, the primary emphasis had been given to the operational systems and the data they process. It is not practical to keep data in the operational systems indefinitely. The fundamental requirements of the operational and analysis systems are different: the operational systems need performance, whereas the analysis systems need flexibility and broad scope. Despite all the changes in the platforms, architectures, tools, and technologies, a remarkably large number of business applications continue to run in the mainframe environment. By some estimates, more than 70 per cent of business data for large corporations still resides in the mainframe environment.

The single biggest challenge in an SEM project is the complexity of the data sources. The firm cannot just buy in an underlying data warehouse; it has to build one, because each warehouse has a unique architecture and a set of requirements that spring from the individual needs of the organisation. The organisation needs to address a wide range of questions in building it. In particular it needs to pay as much attention to the structure, definitions, and flow of data as they do to choosing software. It is important to be aware of the constantly changing needs of their company's

Figure 7.4: The technical architecture of SEM

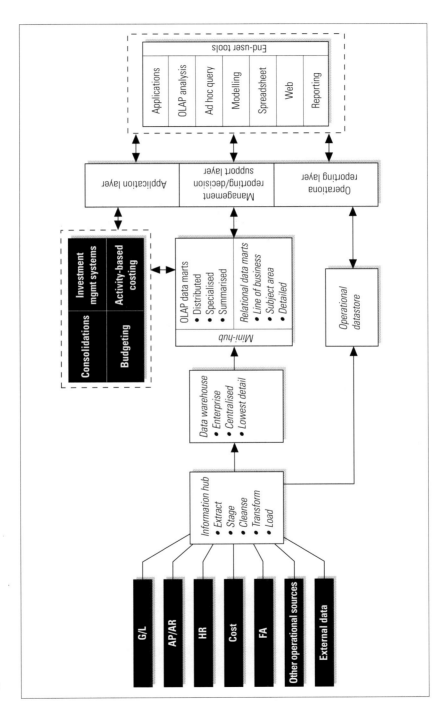

business and the capabilities of the available and emerging technology. Also, there are difficulties in choosing the right products.

Similarly, the underlying data warehouse architecture is expensive to build. One reason data warehouses are so expensive is that data must be moved or copied from existing databases, sometimes manually, and data needs to be translated into a common format. Anecdotal evidence suggests that a lot of data warehousing software still lacks easy to deploy or other standards that shuttle data smoothly through the entire warehouse process.

Data warehousing systems are most successful when data can be combined from more than one operational system. The primary reason for combining data from multiple source applications is the ability to cross-reference data from these applications. Nearly all data in a typical data warehouse is built around the time dimension. The data warehouse system can serve not only as an effective platform to merge data from multiple current applications; but can also integrate multiple versions of the same application.

Before embarking on ambitious and technically demanding projects like data warehouses, it is essential to have an architectural framework. This is a vision of how information systems will be built and deployed in the organisation. In particular it should set out the following:

- how to integrate the different systems both internally and externally;
- how much of the existing ERP vendor SEM functionality to use;
- how much web-based technology should be used;
- how to optimise database/data warehousing capabilities;
- how can integrated, consistent data that can be reconciled to the 'official' financial records be produced;
- how and when should rusting legacy systems be replaced;
- how many new technologies can the firm manage.

In addition the following detailed technical issues need to be considered:

- source data extraction;
- data transformation;
- transfer of data to data warehouse;
- metadata capture;
- data access; and
- data warehouse development process support.

To support efficient, broad deployment across the enterprise, an SEM architecture should endeavour to be fully web-enabled. This means that users – whether finance staff, business managers, or executives – should be able to access the system and the appropriate functions through a web browser. In an ideal setting, it should be possible for any user to be free from both location and machine when using the system. They should be able to use any machine, from any location, providing it has a suitable web browser and there is a suitable connection to the system. In a web-enabled SEM environment, the web interface should allow setting up a complete SEM portal where users can access and easily integrate information from virtually any source or website.

7.3.4 Phase 4: Identify the required SEM analytical tools

During the past decade, the sharply increasing popularity of the personal computer on business desktops has introduced many new options and compelling opportunities for business analysis. The gap between the IS specialists and end user has started to close as finance professionals now have at their fingertips many of the tools required to gain proficiency in the use of spreadsheets for analysis and graphic representation. Advanced users will frequently use desktop database programs that allow them to store and work with the information extracted from the legacy sources. Many desktop reporting and analysis tools are increasingly targeted towards end users and have gained considerable popularity on the desktop.

The Gartner Group predicts that in the future SEM application software implementations will concentrate on extending the standard ERP modules with specialised applications designed to address more specific business problems. In many cases, companies have only implemented a bare bones version of the standard ERP modules, and need to exploit the specialised features of the products to truly improve their business performance. The ERP vendors are going to face increasing demand from their installed base to provide the specialised functionality they have promised. As a result therefore, organisations will need to evaluate SEM analytical application software from vendors that have specialised in a particular vertical industry segment or in a multi-industry business function to date.

Until recently, full blown SEM software applications were not available. Organisations have had to rely on either linking together multiple, discreet applications for planning, reporting, and analysis, or have had to build unsophisticated applications themselves. This build option typically involves using a generic OLAP tool with a spreadsheet program. This requires extensive effort in building and maintaining not only a financially intelligent model, but also the various end user functions required by each part of the SEM process, such as data extraction, scenario planning, and end user ad hoc analysis capabilities.

The following are some characteristics generally associated with effective SEM analytical tools:

- These systems have data in descriptive standard business terms, rather than in cryptic computer fields names. Data names and data structures in these systems are designed for use by non-technical users.
- The data is generally pre-processed with the application of standard business rules such as how to allocate revenue to products, business units, and markets.
- Consolidated views of the data, such as product, customer, and market, are available.
- Although these systems will at times have the ability to drill down to the detail data, rarely are they able to access all the detail data at the same time.
- These systems enable more robust, statistically sound and sophisticated analysis including 'what if', cause and effect, scenario modelling, sensitivity analysis, and multidimensional modelling.

While organisations may not want to simultaneously embrace ABC/M, balanced scorecard and SVM in a single leap it is important to have a long-term roadmap for the type of analysis required. In particular finance professionals need to consider the following:

- Should the firms go for common global analytical applications across the organisation?
- Should it insist on standardised processes and data definitions across SBUs?
- How can it enable sharing of best practices and experience across the different locations with respect to analytical tools?
- How will the analytical applications be incorporated into the company's existing technical environment?
- How can SEM applications improve productivity, increase analysis and provide more robust information?
- How should the decision support applications be deployed?
- Who should have access to the decisions support applications?

Table 7.1 provides a list of the capabilities which SEM analytical applications should encompass.

Table 7.1: SEM analytical application capabilities

Integrated analysis and data access. An SEM analytical application should provide decision support, consolidation, and management reporting and analysis in a single, 'closed-loop' application. Users should be able to swap from one process to the other without having to change environments or move data.

Common data. Using a common data model avoids the hassles and risks of moving data or updating a rule in multiple systems. No effort is required to maintain links and duplicate changes. No time is lost while those changes/movements are made.

Multidimensionality. It supports unlimited business perspectives, e.g. by organisation, cost centre, product, market, or channel; and unlimited members within each dimension. These dimensions must support multiple hierarchies, such as product and channel, while at the same time supporting multiple alternative hierarchies.

Support for different measure types. Measures can be both financial and non-financial.

Support for currency reporting. Often there is a need to support multiple currency perspectives for global planning and reporting. The database must be able to translate accounts at different rates, detect and calculate exchange gains/losses, and then consolidate the results into a base currency or currencies. It must also be able to convert measures at multiple sets of rates and allow the comparison of results to assess the affects of exchange fluctuations.

Flexible level of detail for business intelligence applications. Different BI processes require different levels of detail. For example, strategic plans may occur at a divisional level, budgets at a departmental level, and actuals are collected by product, customer, etc. Where the level of detail coincides, it should be possible to compare data directly.

Communication and collaboration. Users should be able to access data on-line without advance notice, i.e. not as part of a pre-configured report. Users should be able to view and analyse data across any appropriate dimensions, without limitations, such as by initiative, product, line of business, etc. They must also be able to rotate and nest dimensions as well as drill down to lower levels of detail within the model. These drill downs should use the most current structures. When the lowest level of the business model is reached, drill downs should be capable of going back to the underlying data source.

Central database employing scalable, mainstream technology. SEM applications should be built on top of a central database rather than using proprietary file structures that are common in many of today's systems.

7.3.5 *Phase 5: Deploying the SEM capability*

As Figure 7.5 illustrates deploying full SEM capability involves three key areas. Firstly, developing the data extraction loading and data reconciliations needed to populate the business/data warehouse. Secondly, implementing the data warehousing architecture and supporting OLAP software; and finally implementing the SEM analytical applications.

Figure 7.5: Deploying full SEM capability

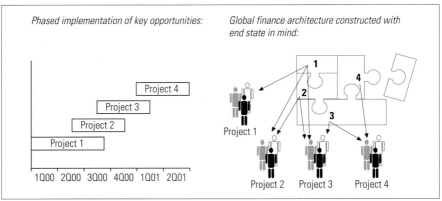

In deciding which applications to deploy, the prioritisation criteria should highlight those opportunities that provide a high return and that can be implemented within a reasonable amount of time. In addition, in implementing the SEM capability the firm must ensure that the phased implementation of the different elements is part of an overall plan. As such the SEM deployment should encompass creating building blocks that achieve the end vision and allow information captured from one project to be leveraged by other projects. In Figure 7.6, each project builds on the previous project to achieve synergies.

7.3.6 *Phase 6: Go-live and support – implement the opportunities*

In this phase the transition from pre-production to a live stable system is made. It involves the rollout of the new SEM system and is the most difficult part of the project. This phase runs from day 1 of going live, to a 'system stable' long-term support environment. By the end of this phase the finance staff will have taken ownership of the new system and the system is running.

Figure 7.6: The SEM software

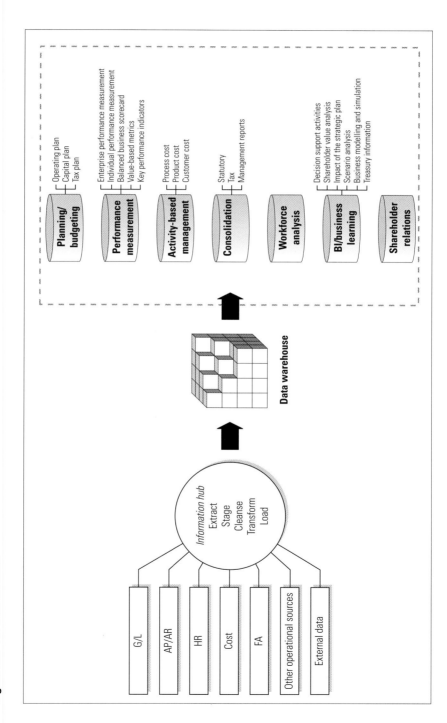

While the go-live phase effectively means the end of the project, the real task of leveraging the benefits of the SEM system begins at the go-live date. In this phase, post go-live activities such as delivering value added analysis to management begins.

7.4 Change management and SEM

In its broadest sense, change management refers to all the non-technological activities that are required during and after the SEM implementation to achieve the desired business benefits. They include: stakeholder management; communications; education and training; benefits management (particularly of the 'intangible', non-quantifiable benefits); culture and organisational change; and resource management (see Figure 7.7 for an example of a change management framework).

Many of the organisations that failed to realise the full benefits of their initial investment in ERP exhibit a degree of scepticism about investing further in enterprise systems. The scepticism is understandable but, very often failure to capitalise fully on the investment was predictable given the organisations' attitudes to people-related impacts of change.

The experience of ERP implementations now shows that the failure of organisations to capitalise fully on the benefits of ERP was often not due to weaknesses in the technological solution. Poor change management often resulted in longer programmes, higher implementation costs and extended periods of stabilisation after go-live, as the 'people' issues ignored during the implementation emerged later.

The management of an SEM implementation in an organisation is intrinsically bound up with change. There is a widespread view that there is more change and greater pressure for quick change than ever before. The technology literature abounds with examples of change projects that have gone wrong, some disastrously so. At the introduction of new technology in the 1980s, when information technology was coming into its own, the failure rate of new technology projects was between 40 and 70 per cent. In the case of ERP, there is evidence to suggest that a vast number of projects fail to deliver the expected benefits.

Failure rates such as these are sobering. In individual cases people put the blame on personalities or poor workplace relations, if change is not going well. However, a failure rate of 70 per cent suggests it would be better to look hard at how well the change business is understood and how well it is managed. Effective change management lies at the heart of successful SEM deployment. However, effective change management is not

Figure 7.7: Example of a change management framework.

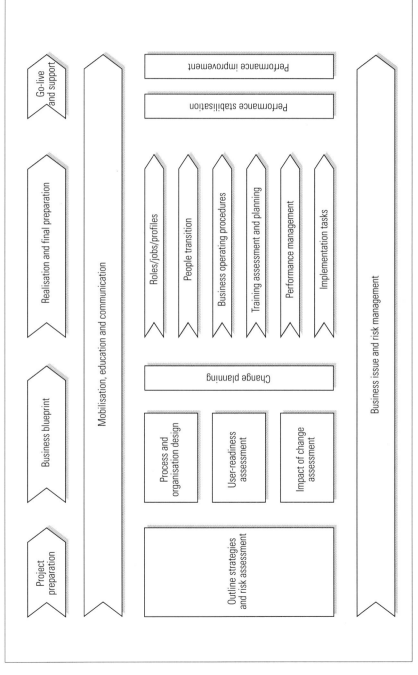

© Partners for Change Ltd. 2001.

easy and demands a substantial organisational commitment and top management support. It means helping the organisation get information on its current position. It means helping it make sense of what success means for it and putting this into a new framework. Skilful steering of the process is required, including knowing how to manage resistance to change in an appropriate way.

Partners for Change Ltd., a leading consultancy specialising in ERP-type implementations, has identified a number of issues with respect to change management in the context of enterprise systems:

- *Technology led:* In many enterprise systems project managers allowed technology to drive the programme. In the case of a substantial number of ERP projects IT management took the lead, especially where ERP was just a technical solution (to Year 2000 compliance, for example). End users and their managers were often insufficiently involved in scoping, planning and running the programme.

- *Unrealistic timescales:* Many systems implementations are driven to very tight deadlines. Where organisations lack the capability to implement the technology or the changes that go with it, there is insufficient time to build an effective internal team.

- *Weak business cases:* The bandwagon effect can mean that organisations decide to implement ERP because their competitors are, without looking closely at their own business case. As a result insufficient attention is paid to managing projects towards the delivery of benefits.

- *Incomplete strategy:* Many companies aim to implement systems quickly against existing working practices and then start process improvements that delivered benefits over time. The initial implementation tends to be faster and less disruptive than attempting to re-design the process as part of the initial implementation. The benefits are delivered later. While this can be perceived to be a less risky approach, in practice, many companies fail to establish the process improvement programme that will deliver the benefits, usually for reasons of cost or time pressure.

- *Management overload:* The combination of multiple concurrent change initiatives can result in 'overload' on senior management, as their number and complexity increase, and managers attempt to balance competing calls on their attention. Communications often break down, in turn resulting in poor decision-making, internal conflict and confusion.

- *Stakeholders:* Senior management overload resulting from the multiplicity of initiatives often also means that the most important stakeholders are insufficiently involved in scoping and planning the programme. Their full commitment is not engendered, and even when it is, their attention is often later re-directed to other initiatives.
- *Inadequate resources and skills:* Multiple change initiatives invariably compete for resources from a finite internal pool. Funding may not be available to bring in sufficient temporary, external support. This is often compounded by managers' reluctance to dedicate full-time resources from the line to support programmes and projects that are not considered to be 'real' work.

Polly Schneider in an article called 'ERPeople Skills' in *CIO Magazine* identified a number of what she called cultural hot spots which need to be addressed as part of enterprise systems implementations.

7.5 Key lessons going forward

To date many systems implementations have been treated as technology projects and not business driven transformations. Approaching the implementation from an IS perspective often leads to attempts to try to tie down all of the major requirements at an early stage with large disincentives for changing these at a later stage. As a result many firms have found themselves trapped in a technological straightjacket solution which ignores the dynamic, evolutionary nature of SEM implementations and the business environment. If long-term competitive advantage from SEM systems is to be achieved, it requires the on-going commitment of senior executives to the project. The failure of senior project sponsors to remain involved in a project will result in the project team loosing sight of the business nature of the implementation and allow it to become an IT project. Project sponsors/champions must not only provide the resources for the implementation but they must also take an active role in leading change. In particular, they must create the emotional climate for change and be proactive in building co-operation among the diverse groups on the implementation team and throughout the organisation.

7.5.1 The right executive sponsor

The importance of having an executive sponsor at the right level of seniority cannot be over-stated. If the whole company is affected, then it should be the CFO who sponsors the programme. The CFO should be the champion at board level. As executive sponsors CFOs need to understand what influence they have, how to exert it and how to get involved.

7.5.2 Clarify the role of other stakeholders

Other groups outside of the finance function have a legitimate role to play in the SEM project. This includes IT specialists, strategic planning groups, functional area data providers and senior business managers, who are not involved in the day-to-day of SEM, but who are nevertheless affected by it.

7.5.3 Develop an explicit strategy for benefits realisation

More, intangible, 'strategy-related' benefits will need to have a higher profile in the business cases for SEM implementations, especially those that relate to improved business learning and direction setting. The business case for SEM needs to be driven by those who will be accountable for implementation and delivery of the benefits. Buy-in from the key stakeholders in each of the key areas is essential. Having made people accountable, it is important to get them involved in the programme in a meaningful way so that they can influence it. The consequences of failing to get this buy-in will result in longer implementations and potential failure to deliver the benefits. SEM benefits need to be managed in a careful and systematic way and it is important that the SEM implementation references the strategic direction of the business to ensure that the system continually supports the business objectives. Benefits identified should be measurable and quantifiable so that organisations have a basis for prioritisation. Opportunities for benefit need to be filtered to determine where the best value can be obtained. As such the organisation needs to adopt a structured approach and ask two basic questions:

1. What is the initial business case and how will we deliver the expected benefit?
2. How can we leverage the SEM technology we have to deliver more benefits?

7.5.4 Look for quick wins

These are benefits that are readily available from the current SEMs capability, but are not yet realised. Normally these benefits can be achieved relatively easily with minimal effort. Their value is partly in allowing the organisation to start to re-coup some of the programme cost fairly soon after the start. More importantly, these gains should help to build credibility in the programme and perhaps bolster the case for continued investment.

7.5.5 *Beware the valley of death*

It is now recognised that most organisations experience a 'dip' in performance immediately after go-live with SEM. Change management processes during and after roll-out and cutover have a key role to play in minimising this 'dip' by:

● engendering a smooth 'go-live';
● minimising the effect on normal reporting operations; and
● achieving rapid stabilisation after 'go-live'.

Figure 7.8 *Performance 'dip' after 'go-live' in SEM*

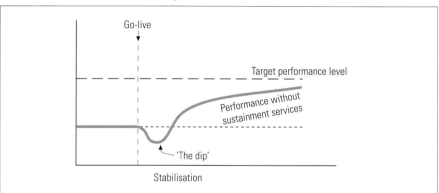

7.5.6 *Get the right participants*

One of the key components of well-managed change is the level of participation gained through implementation. When there has been inadequate participation from the business, the quality of the solution is often poor. In order to get people to take ownership of the solution it is important to get the right people from the business involved from the start. If they have an input to the design, development and the overall strategy behind the SEM project, they will be more supportive post 'go-live' thus reducing the dip in productivity. If they are not involved, there may be a prolonged period of reduced productivity with detrimental effects on the business reporting.

7.5.7 *Resource management and capability transfer*

As part of the programme planning process, resource skill requirements should be defined, current capabilities assessed, gaps identified, and training provided. Where resource shortages are identified – within the SEM team – plans will need to be constructed to bridge the gaps. Formal plans should also be established and managed to transfer key skills from any external consulting resources to the organisation's own staff.

7.5.8 *Other advice*

- View the SEM implementation as a business initiative, not an IS initiative.
- Educate and engage senior management about SEM as early as possible.
- Do not let technical problems dominate the project's time.
- Avoid political infighting between previously isolated divisions.
- Do not change too much at once
- Do not overwhelm the organisation with a system that has more functionality than it absolutely needs.
- Consider a phased rollout and shoot for short wins to generate momentum during the project.

There are also some guiding principles for effective team behaviour that extend beyond cultural or physical boundaries, these include mutual respect for team members' cultures and working practices; a focus on solutions rather than problems and no recriminations ('finger pointing') when things go wrong. While a detailed discussion of these issues is beyond the scope of this chapter it is clear that SEM implementation requires a wider understanding of change management and cultural issues than many practitioners have demonstrated to date.

Future directions and challenges

8

8.1 Introduction

Organisations are faced with the challenge of continuing to deliver value to shareholders, while at the same time managing the complex multiple partner relationships which characterise the emerging e-business driven value chain. In order to successfully leverage their investment in SEM, firms must recognise that SEM is an entirely different type of systems investment. In particular, they need to recognise that the value of SEM is inherently tied to managers' ability to use it to design and configure a continually evolving business model.

Figure 8.1: Strategic management activities

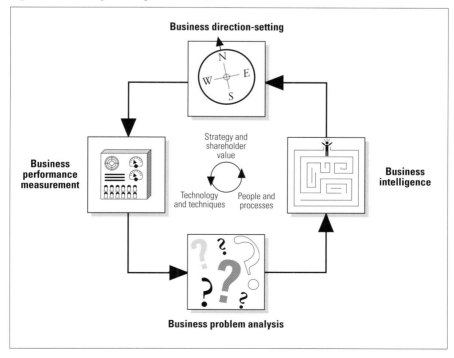

As the pace of business speeds up, firms are searching for innovative ways to access information, enter new markets, gain new sources of revenue and increase productivity. A flexible and robust SEM capability which is aligned with the firm's business model is a prerequisite for competing in the world of e-business.

In the past firms typically relied on single vendor solutions to meet their decision support requirements. In the future firms will need to become more comfortable with the notion of best of breed solutions and develop the vendor relationship management and integration skills to implement the best available solutions for particular functionality.

To realise the full benefits of SEM, however, requires more than just technical insight. Instead successful SEM deployment in pursuit of shareholder value requires a careful balancing of vision, resources, creativity and above all a superior understanding of the competitive landscape.

8.2 E-everything

Internet technology is transforming business processes, helping firms build new relationships with customers, suppliers, and partners, and channelling information for effective enterprise-wide decision-making. Forward-looking companies need to harness the power of the web to improve the finance processes. In particular firms can use the web to:

● reduce the cost of the finance department;
● take cost out of the business processes;
● speed up or eliminate the monthly closing cycle;
● improve the quality of source data; and
● customise information for decision-makers using portals enabling better decision-making.

As Figure 8.2 illustrates the web will play a key role in the information technology of firms at all levels. At the core operations level the web will facilitate B2B, B2C and B2E self-service activities. These will become the key data sources for much of the internal information used in SEM applications. In many cases processes which are currently labour intensive, such as invoice processing and fulfilment, will take place in highly automated e-shared service centres which will act as e-business hubs for much of the day-to-day transaction processing.

Figure 8.2: The emerging IT architecture

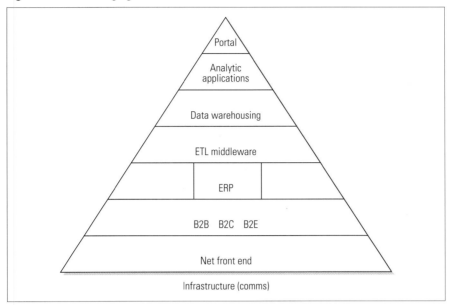

At the strategic level portal technology will be used to deliver uniquely customised and flexible interfaces for decision-makers which may in time be incorporated into emerging mobile computing platforms. Executives will be able to tailor their desktop to reflect their immediate decision-making concerns in a way which allows them to align their decision support with their changing management agenda. Before this can happen, however, firms need to address a number of key challenges with respect to the finance systems:

- Select SEM platforms and tools that support varying needs of different users and which allow the linking of multiple data 'cubes' across many dimensions and at multiple levels.
- Deliver SEM systems implementations in short cycles.
- Develop a wider organisational knowledge of SEM tools, processes and data definitions.
- Move towards a common but pluralistic SEM architecture that is web enabled from the source systems to the executive desktop.
- Find mechanisms to incorporate the emerging SEM tools into the existing technical architecture and infrastructure.

- Find ways of using the SEM tools to improve productivity, increase analysis and provide more robust information.
- Produce integrated, consistent data that can be reconciled back to the 'official' published financial records.
- Manage the evaluation, selection and implementation of a continuous stream of SEM software products.
- Leverage early prototyping and piloting to accelerate delivery and increase the awareness and support for SEM.
- Develop appropriate organisational mechanisms for deploying the SEM applications.
- Develop approaches which allow emerging SEM and other technologies to be incorporated into the SEM architecture.
- Develop robust, end-to-end processes for SEM which allow the firm to transform data into information.
- Synchronise SEM activities across the organisation.
- Reduce the reliance on existing hard copy paper-based reporting, by deploying more cost-effective web-enabled tools and decommissioning existing decision support systems where appropriate.

The next five years will see the emergence of a mature e-SEM technology environment in which processes, data, customers, suppliers, employees and other stakeholders are integrated in real time. If SEM technologies are to achieve their promise we must recognise that they are evolving and continuously changing technologies that must be managed proactively. Management accountants must continue to embrace these technologies enthusiastically and take a proactive role in deploying them in pursuit of improved business analysis and planning. In the future accountants will be increasingly involved in configuring and deploying not just new business processes but also new business models. In this regard management accounting may finally begin to fulfil its strategic potential in organisations.

8.2.1 People and processes

In the very near future firms must start to make the transition to web-enabled finance processes. As Figure 8.3 illustrates this will see the emergence of highly automated transaction processing with business controls embedded in the systems. With accountants freed from the drudgery of routine transaction processing they can start to focus on:

- reducing closing times with integrated general ledger, consolidation, and reporting tools;
- aligning top-down business planning with performance metrics and detailed budgeting;
- performing more analysis and less manual data collection, manipulation, and reconciliation; and
- delivering decision support information instead of monitoring performance.

Figure 8.3: Web-enabled finance processes

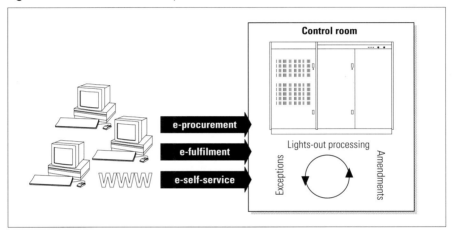

As part of the move towards this new finance culture, accountants will have to accept the important role which non-professionally qualified 'accountants' can make. In particular engineers, marketing experts, and others who have operations experience (perhaps supplemented by an MBA) will in the future play an important role in delivering the SEM capability firms need. If SEM is to address the broad range of strategic issues, the finance function needs to broaden its skill base to include those with the core business insight. In addition, accountants will have to spend time in non-accounting front line customer-facing value creation roles.

If finance professionals are to deliver on the promise of SEM, then they need to shed the scorekeeper/'number cruncher' and 'bean counter' stereotype and start to be perceived as business partners. As part of their SEM role, finance professionals will need to spend more time communicating with people in other functional areas and good interpersonal skills will be essential for success. Increasingly finance staff will be expected to carry out their role as SEM providers outside the accounting function at the front line of operational divisions, where the decision points are. Research indicates that to date only about 50 per cent of finance professionals do this effectively at present. Finance professionals have an opportunity to take the lead in deploying SEM and this will require them to spend time working in cross functional teams and, unusually for many, as project team leaders. In order to deliver on the SEM vision, finance staff will need to find creative ways of:

● increasing the amount of analysis and decision support they provide;
● increasing their contribution to non-traditional accounting activities in particular forward-looking activities such as strategic planning, internal consulting, process improvement, and performance evaluation; and
● driving down the time spent on standardised financial reports, accounting systems, short-term budgeting, project accounting, compliance reporting accounting policy, and consolidations issues.

The real key to making a successful transition to the business partner role will occur when finance staff begin to deliver improved support for the strategic business decisions that are being made. As such, strategic planning and process improvement will be the two most critical work activities. To succeed in this environment firms will have to select, develop and retain a pool of new finance professionals who have:

● the ability to communicate well, orally and in writing;
● the ability to work in a team and encourage openness and sharing of best practice;
● strong analytical skills and a solid understanding of accounting;
● the skills to apply a consultative approach to deploying SEM tools;
● the facilitation skills to coach and support other team members; and
● an appreciation of value rather than cost and a solid understanding of how a business functions in terms of strong commercial acumen.

Most of all it requires CFOs who are strategic, proactive, forward-looking visionaries who can share organisational decision-making and business execution with their CEO. It requires a finance culture which understands the value imperative and one in which the focus is on insight, execution and delivery of business benefits.

Effective change management lies at the heart of successful SEM deployment. However, effective change management is not easy and demands a substantial organisational commitment and top management support. It means helping the organisation get information on its current position. It means helping it make sense of what success means for it and putting this into a new framework. This involves bringing together the change concept and the current organisational context and asking hard questions as to why the one should work for the other. It means creating a structure to manage the transition between the existing situation and the new situation and setting up that structure in a way that maximises its chances of success. Skilful steering of the process is required, including knowing how to manage resistance to change in an appropriate way. If long-term competitive advantage from SEM is to be achieved, it requires the on-going commitment of senior executives to the project. The failure of senior project sponsors to remain involved in a project will result in the project team loosing sight of the business nature of the implementation and allow it to become an IT project. Project sponsors/champions must not only provide the resources for the implementation but they must also take an active role in leading change. In particular, they must create the emotional climate for change and be proactive in building co-operation among the diverse groups on the implementation team and throughout the organisation, often across national boundaries.

8.2.2 *Strategy and shareholder value – the value imperative*

The last three years has seen the coming together of two of the key technologies of the last decade: ERP systems and the world wide web. Firms have quickly realised that a successful business model requires a stable and robust underlying transaction and information processing infrastructure. In addition firms have recognised that to effectively exploit the opportunities of the web they needed to have superior information and knowledge-based processes. As a result a strong SEM capability will be increasingly important for a successful e-business.

The Internet has fundamentally changed competitive strategies and business processes, transforming traditional business models to more efficient, more flexible e-business models. As industries become deregulated and privatised, and companies extend their reach to global markets, competition for customers increases at a dramatic rate. Large firms in particular can be susceptible to low cost competition from so called virtual firms. Without the heavy burden of investment in fixed assets, smaller and leaner virtual operators are able to undercut traditional operators, particularly in the business to consumer market for items such as CDs, books, airline tickets, etc. Established market leaders that do not seize the on-line opportunity may lose market share to start-ups emerging from nowhere.

Increasingly strategy formulation and execution has become an on-going preoccupation for executives. In particular, firms are recognising that it is no longer sufficient for an organisation to revisit its strategic plan once or twice a year to compare actual versus projected performance. The complexity and competitiveness of the e-business environment requires a more dynamic approach to enterprise management than many firms have adopted in the past. If firms are to create significant shareholder value, they need mechanisms which allow them to collect distributed budgeting and planning data from front-line managers, and consolidate that data along with other pertinent internal and external information into a centralised resource for strategic management of the enterprise. In the absence of this information senior management are forced to rely on ad hoc and often spreadsheet-based IT solutions in their attempts to craft the strategic plan and fine-tune that plan in the face of changes in capital markets and competitor actions.

The next five years will see an unprecedented change in managers' decision-support expectations and an increasing requirement for flexible management accounting and control systems. If the finance function is to meet this challenge and survive (and not go the way of industrial engineers), it is essential that they have access to, and can share, first rate information and analysis tools, and that they make good use of genuine empowerment to shape lasting solutions to fundamental problems. A key part of this will be moving beyond the notion that it is enough to merely make information available. Information must be provided in a way that encourages organisational collaboration and shared meaning. The end objective, therefore, is not a smoothing over of disparities in opinion or the pursuit of a single absolute meaning, but instead a shared insight into the complexity of the problem being faced.

In the past the information contained in ERP systems has been used primarily for surveillance purposes rather than decision-making. ERP systems which have formed the bulk of IS activity in organisations have been primarily concerned with the early intelligence phase of decision-making. In addition, the systems have had a strong tracking and control bias. The ERP systems implemented have tended to focus on data gathering and processing and played little role in meeting the ad hoc support associated with decision support. Support for the design and choice phases of decision-making has relied primarily on end-user developed, spreadsheet-based decision support systems. With the emerging SEM tools finance staff have an opportunity to interact with their information systems in a much richer way than is provided by ERP systems and in a more robust way than with spreadsheet tools.

A key starting point in any attempt to improve the management support capabilities of SEM systems is to get a better understanding of senior executives' modelling and analysis activities and, in particular, to get a better understanding of the ways in which they interact with the information currently held in the organisational systems.

Under conventional approaches to strategic management many firms have failed to redesign the reporting and performance management systems to take account of the primacy of stakeholders. Many of the approaches currently in place reflect a bottom line profitability perspective rather than a value perspective. As a result the rhetoric of value management is not matched by the reality of performance management systems and business execution. This has two major consequences. Firstly, management is not driving the business towards value maximisation and secondly, there is an increasing mismatch between external and internal information reporting systems.

Business performance measurement and control has been the focus of many of the innovations in management in the last ten years. Techniques and systems such as ERP, ABC/M, balanced scorecard, consolidation software, EIS, strategic budgeting, and strategic cost management have all attempted to address the information deficit facing managers in this area. Business performance measurement is concerned primarily with monitoring the results of past decisions in an attempt to provide management accountants, product managers, corporate centres and others with an early warning system for business problems. As such, the focus is primarily on evaluating the performance of SBUs and operating sites against specific targets. The SEM approach seeks to effectively link performance measurement and control to strategic objectives, in an attempt to ensure that operational decision-making is fully focused on delivering strategic objectives. Under SEM the drivers of stakeholder value are the key performance evaluation criteria and the traditional approaches to performance measurement and control are extended to include competitors, customers, products and relative market position. SEM thus attempts to support decision-makers' information needs, provides seamless integration of strategic, financial and operational information and provides transparency across the enterprise to ensure continuity of information from strategy through to execution (see Figure 8.4). As the number of individuals involved in the strategic management process increases, and the amount of strategic management increases, it is critical that the quality of that process is improved. SEM improves the quality of the strategic management process by providing managers with the data, information and analysis capability to explore strategic issues in a richer and more effective way than before.

Transforming information into effective business decisions requires SEM-based solutions that provide timely and accurate access to information to support the key strategic management activities. SEM capability needs to be firmly focused on improving the effectiveness of strategic management processes by providing managers with business performance monitoring, consolidation, and data warehousing/business intelligence capability. As such, SEM should be concerned with improving the strategy formulation/execution process and with helping organisations measure and manage performance and shareholder value in a wide variety of ways, and then distributing the results in comprehensible, usable formats.

As discussed earlier the insights which managers use in solving complex problems are based on individual and organisational knowledge. Managers use intuition, judgement, and trial and error to find solutions. Much of the knowledge managers use is held as unrecorded impressions and insights in the heads of individuals. As problem complexity increases there is a greater need for extensive inputs from diverse specialists, and clarification of goals. For managers thinking is inseparable from acting, with managers developing an understanding by thinking and acting in close concert. Problem analysis is not a passive process but a dynamic, interactive series of activity and reflection. In many situations, managers simply cannot determine or predict which alternative will solve a problem. Intuition, judgement, trial and error are used to find solutions. In many cases, the 'learning is in the doing'. In these situations executives require systems to support decision-making which have the following characteristics:

- immediate to the activity (i.e. developed by trusted support staff);
- concrete descriptions of the unique situations (informed by business acumen);
- concise, cursory and diffuse (simple, effective reflections of executives mental models);
- representations of the actual processes (no wild constraining assumptions as with OR models); and
- connection of the performance to the processes in the situation (reflect real processes).

Figure 8.4: The SEM process.

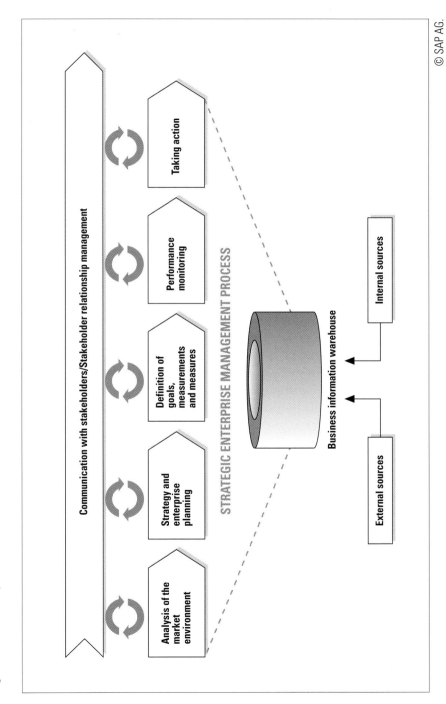

In the future SEM offers many opportunities for finance professionals to move to the centre of information and knowledge-based processes in
the organisation. Businesses of the 21st century must have management
processes in place to monitor and control the organisation, while at the
same time decentralising decision-making in order to react to competitive
changes and take advantage of unexpected opportunities. One central
element that supports this balance between control and flexibility is shared
knowledge. Such knowledge, derived from both internal and external data
sources, is converted to information that can be readily interpreted.

Long-term advantage from SEM will come not from the adoption of
standardised technological solutions, but from the creation of an SEM
capability which recognises the inherent flexibility/uncertainty and ambiguity of the manager's environment. The focus needs to shift to providing
an environment which allows managers to interact in a richer way with
information and to make more explicit the tacit mental models of the business which managers have.

If SEM is to make a lasting impact on strategic management processes
it must be recognised that the provision of information processing and analysis capabilities is only a small part of improving decision-making. SEM technology offerings must explicitly recognise that even sophisticated modelling
and statistical techniques are of limited value where managers are faced by
highly novel problem situations where their ability to specify the variables
involved is constrained. SEM also needs to take cognisance of the fact the
strategic problems require diverse inputs from inter-disciplinary teams.

If SEM is to be successful in supporting business problem solving at
the strategic level it must go beyond providing managers with access to the
technology and data they need and instead address the issues of tools for
improving problem definition, problem analysis, alternative evaluation
and choice. In particular, SEM needs to improve the manager's ability to
leverage insights and share tacit knowledge by drawing on the principles
of knowledge management and organisational learning. SEM needs to provide management with a continuous learning environment in which managers are equipped with the knowledge and insight to react quickly and
effectively to the changing strategic challenges. In particular, SEM should
be extended to provide managers with support in:

- sharing individual insights and organisational knowledge;
- using intuition, judgement, trial and error to find solutions;
- managing extensive inputs from diverse specialists; and
- developing complex mental models of their problem space.

8.3 Concluding remarks

It is not clear that the SEM technology offerings to date are capable of bringing about the long-term changes needed to institutionalise these practices. In particular, SEM offerings to date need to be more informed by the organisational change and the decision support literature.

The evidence from previous research in the area of decision support systems suggests that the technology and techniques are just one element in successful performance. In particular, it has been shown that SEM personnel and the SEM process are an equally important part of improving decision-making. It can be argued that from a technological perspective there is very little new in SEM. Many of the applications/tools reflect functionality previously seen in EIS, data warehousing and modelling software. The technology and techniques which make up the SEM offerings from vendors are perfectly replicable and widely documented in the public domain and are likely to be copied by mid-market ERP vendors in the near future. In addition, the SEM strategy of all of the major vendors appears to be based on a very rational/planned model of organisational strategy. In particular, it assumes the existence of an articulable set of business models. If SEM is to make a lasting impact at the strategic level, it must be done within a framework which codifies, in a coherent but flexible approach, a set of organisational interventions designed to leverage management insights and understanding through the use of SEM technologies and techniques. While the SEM technologies will remain largely the domain of established enterprise systems vendors, the successful implementation of SEM will require a much richer understanding of the nature of strategic management and an understanding of the decision support process.

As traditional custodians of the firms performance measurement and control systems, finance professionals have in the past taken a mainly functional internal perspective on decision support systems. In the future the challenge is for them to move beyond their traditional role as scorekeepers to one in which they are actively participating in the design and deployment of new business models. A key role in this business model redesign and deployment will be ensuring that the organisations information and transaction processing systems are aligned with and support the evolving business model. In this sense finance professionals are challenged to take ownership and responsibility for the SEM initiative and ensure they generate the shareholder value they promised.

Bibliography

Arthur Andersen LLP and Scott, T. (1998), *Case Study: Using Packaged Analytic Applications to maximise the value of ERP.*

Arthur Andersen (1999), *STOXX 50 Shareholder Value and Investor Relations in Capital Investments*, p. 8.

Ashton, C. (1997), *Strategic Performance Measurement*, London: Business Intelligence.

Barnard, C. I. (1938), *The Functions of the Executive*, Cambridge, Ma: Harvard University Press.

Charan, R. and Colvin, G. (1999), 'Why CEO's fail', *Fortune*, 21 Jun.

Chenhall, R. (1999) 'Reasons for innovation', *Australian CPA*, Oct 1999, Vol. 69, Iss. 9, p. 75.

Cooper, R. (1987), 'Does your company need a cost system?', *Journal of Cost Management*, Spring.

Cooper, R. (1989), 'You need a new cost system when...', *Harvard Business Review*, Jan.

Davenport, T. (1998), 'Putting the enterprise into the enterprise system', *Harvard Business Review*, Vol. 76, No. 4, Jul./Aug., pp. 121–31.

Driver, M. J. and Mock, T. J. (1975), 'Human information processing decision style theory and accounting information systems', *The Accounting Review*, Jul., pp. 490–508.

Ernst and Young (1998), Low, J., and Siesfeld, T., 'Measures that matter', *Strategy and Leadership*, Mar./Apr., p. 24.

Evans, H., Ashworth, G., Gooch, J. and Davies, R. (1996) 'Who needs performance management?', *Management Accounting* (UK), Dec. 1996, p20–25.

FINPLUS 98 International Centre for Business Administration (1998), Conference Papers, Advanced Finance Function Strategies Conference, Amsterdam, Mar. 1998.

Gendron, M. (1997), 'Using the balanced scorecard', *Harvard Management Update*, Oct., pp. 3–5.

Hackathorn, R. (1995), 'Data warehouse energizes your enterprise', *Datamation*, Vol. 41, No.2, (February 1995), pp. 38–45.

Harper, S. C. (1989), 'Intuition: What separates executives from managers', in Agor, W. H. (ed.) *Intuition in Organisations: Leading and Managing Productively*, London: Sage Publications.

Hax, A. C. (1987), *Planning Strategies that Work*, New York: Oxford University Press Inc.

Hussain. S. (1996), 'What do segmental definitions tell us?', *Accountancy*, June 1996, Vol. 117, Iss. 1234 , p. 78.

Inmon, W. H. (1996), *Building the Data Warehouse*, 2nd edn, New York: John Wiley & Sons.

Kaplan, R. S. (1995), 'New roles for management accountants', Journal of Cost Management, Fall, p. 13.

Kaplan, R. S. and Cooper, R. (1998), *Cost and Effect: Using Integrated Cost Systems to Drive Profitability and Performance*, Boston Ma: Harvard Business School Press.

Kaplan, R. S. and Norton, D. P. (1992), 'The balanced scorecard – measures that drive performance', *Harvard Business Review*, Jan.–Feb., pp. 71–79.

Kaplan, R. S. and Norton, D. P. (1996a), 'Using the balanced scorecard as a strategic management system', *Harvard Business Review*, Jan.–Feb., pp. 75–85.

Kaplan, R.S., and Norton, D.P. (1996b), *The Balanced Scorecard: Translating Strategy into Action*, Boston Ma: Harvard Business School Press.

Manning, K. H. (1995), 'Distribution channel profitability', *Management Accounting* (US), Jan.

Mintzberg, H. (1993), *The Rise and Fall of Strategic Planning: Reconceiving Roles for Planning, Plans, Planners*, New York: Free Press.

Myrtveit, M. and Bean, M. (2000), 'Business modelling and simulation', *Wirtschafts Informatik*, special print, Vol. 2, No. 42, Apr.

Norton, D. (1996), *Building a management system to implement your strategy*, Renaissance Solution.

Phillips, G. (1996), 'The future structure of the finance function', *Management Accounting* (UK), Feb. 1996, pp. 12–13.

Polanyi, M. (1967), *The Tacit Dimension*, Garden City, NY: Doubleday.

Quinn, J. (1980), *Strategies for Change: Logical Incrementalism*, Toronto: Irwin.

Rappaport, A. (1997), *Creating Shareholder Value: A Guide for Managers and Investors*, New York: Free Press.

Ross G, (1990), *Management Accounting* (UK), Nov.

Sakaguchi, T. and Frolick, M.N. (1997), 'A review of the data warehousing literature', *Journal of DataWarehousing*, Vol. 2, No. 1, Jan., pp. 34–54.

Schneider, P. (1999), 'Wanted: ERpeople skills', *CIO Magazine*, 1 Mar.

Steiner, G. (1997), *Strategic Planning: What Every Manager Must Know*, New York: The Free Press.

Tate Bramald Consultancy (November 1996), *Report on Management Accountants' use of IT.*

Treacy, M. and Wiersema, F. (1996), *The Discipline of Market Leaders: Choose Your Customers, Narrow Your Focus, Dominate Your Market*, New York: Perseus Publishing.

Tregoe, B. B. and Zimmerman, J.W. (1983), *Top Management Strategy: What it is and How to Make it Work*, New York: Simon & Schuster.

Turney P. B. (1991a), *Common Cents – the ABC Performance Breakthrough the ABC Performance Breakthrough,* Portland, OR: Cost Technology Inc.

Turney P. B. (1991b), 'How ABC helps reduce cost', *Journal of Cost Management*, Winter.

Wefers, M. (2000), 'Strategic enterprise management with the balanced scorecard', *Wirtschafts Informatik*, special print, Vol. 2, No. 42, Apr.

Index

List of figures

List of tables